Zigzag

A Life of Reading and Writing, Teaching and Learning

Tom Romano

HEINE
Portsmc

Heinemann
361 Hanover Street
Portsmouth, NH 03801–3912
www.heinemann.com

Offices and agents throughout the world

The author and publisher wish to thank those who have generously given permission to reprint borrowed material:

"The Danger of Countenance" by Tom Romano was originally published in *English Journal* (Volume 92, Number 6, 2003). Copyright © 2003 by the National Council of Teachers of English. Reprinted with permission.

"I know that he exists" by Emily Dickinson. Reprinted by permission of the publishers and the Trustees of Amherst College from *The Poems of Emily Dickinson*, Thomas H. Johnson, ed., Cambridge, Mass.: The Belknap Press of Harvard University Press. Copyright © 1951, 1955, 1979, 1983 by the President and Fellows of Harvard College.

Acknowledgments for borrowed material continue on page 210.

Photograph of author in Chapter 13 by Scott Kissell. Photograph of author on Part 4 by Anne Koch Jantzen. Photograph of author and Donald Graves in Chapter 29 by Alan Frager. Photograph of author on Part 5 by Bill Hicks. Photograph of author and Donald Murray on Part 6 by Debbie Plater.

Cataloging-in-Publication data is on file at the Library of Congress.
ISBN-13: 978-0-325-01125-7
ISBN-10: 0-325-01125-7

Editor: Lisa Luedeke
Production: Vicki Kasabian
Cover design: Judy Arisman
Author's photograph: Kathy Romano
Typesetter: Publishers' Design and Production Services, Inc.
Manufacturing: Steve Bernier

Printed in the United States of America on acid-free paper
12   11   10   09   08   VP   1   2   3   4   5

To Bill Strong

Emeritus Professor, Utah State University
Writer of intellect, grace, and insight
Friend and Kauaian companion for my words

Contents

Prolog You Won't Want to Skip   vii

Part 1: Growing Up, Taking Shape

1: My Father's Voice   3
2: The Place   5
3: Neighbors   12
4: Home Office   20
5: Phone Call   24
6: Surrealism   26
7: Argument   30
8: Solace   33
9: The Visit   37
10: The Greatest Book   39
11: Church Teaching, Church Learning   42
12: The Danger of Countenance   49

Part 2: College

13: Wayward Beginning   61
14: Making the Grade   65
15: Exam   68
16: Enter Whitman   74
17: Milton   79
18: Coming to Teaching   82
19: Living Literature   90

Part 3: Teaching in High School

20: Moral Outrage   95
21: Over the Hump   101
22: Thriving   106
23: Zeal   112
24: Menagerie   117
25: Soaring   124
26: Making Plans   128

Part 4: UNH

27: Giants   135
28: Meltdown   144
29: Final Assignment   149

Part 5: Reentry

30: Reentry   157
31: Clearing the Way   163
32: Publication   168
33: The Way I'd Like to Teach   174
34: Of Whitman and Friend   177
35: Multigenre   180
36: Clear Decision   185
37: A Good Run Done   187

Part 6: UNH Reprise

38: Indiana Tumble   193
39: Digging In   195
40: Pure Pleasure   201

Epilog: Almost There   *205*

Works Cited   *207*

Gratitudes   *211*

Prolog You Won't Want to Skip

I sat outside a motel entrance on a sunny Saturday morning in Texarkana, awaiting my ride from an associate of the North Texas Writing Project. In the parking lot a multigenerational family unloaded its van. Adults and children milled about, talking and stretching, the father piling luggage onto a wheeled cart. The stack grew high and heavy. One of the children—a girl about seven—insisted on pushing the cart into the motel lobby. The father wasn't inclined to let her. She made her case, he countered, they jousted, he relented. She took the cart's handle and pushed, leaning in, grunting—not a budge. Her father gave the cart a shove, and the girl was off, straining against the weight to keep the cart moving as it veered this way and that, she frantically adjusting her balance and positioning.

"Stop zigzagging!" her mother said.

Behind her, the grandmother called, "She doin' the best she can."

There's my life, I thought, and jotted the bones of the incident in my journal.

I am not a natural-born teacher. I am not a writer of ease and facility. I've done a lot of zigzagging to get where I am: teacher of writing for thirty-seven years, writer of essays, sketches, book reviews, poems, and occasional books. Sometimes my writing and teaching work, and I gain publications and strong teaching evaluations. Sometimes they don't work, and I get rejections and feelings of regret from poorly taught lessons. I have to rethink, replan, revise. Adjusting my balance and positioning is ongoing.

The scene in that motel parking lot represents two extreme views of teaching and learning. One values performance above all else: Standards must be met, period. Benchmarks must be set, every performance tested, measured, and judged. No zigzagging! The other view of learning values growth and development. Its watchword is *approximation*. Teachers who value approximation know that learners will be more accomplished tomorrow than they are today. Amid darkness, these teachers find light and use that light to illuminate possibility. They believe that if learners participate in good faith and keep an eye on the teetering load while moving toward the destination, they will accomplish things they can be proud of. They will be doin' the best they can.

This memoir is grounded in experience and emotion. Specific people, times, places, and incidents combined to create indelible moments that have stayed with me for years. Reading and writing—those flip sides of the literacy coin—often rounded those indelible moments. My life as teacher and writer evolved from them. Sometimes I knew the meaning of an experience I wanted to render. Sometimes I didn't. Only through writing did meaning come clear.

I want you to understand and maybe even experience my development as reader, writer, teacher, and learner. I hope you learn something, as I have. Sometimes, to my chagrin, that learning will be counterlessons to how I have proceeded. I've orchestrated incredible flub-ups that I hope you avoid. I've made rash decisions and gross miscalculations. I've often missed what should have been obvious. I hope, too, though, that you learn something directly from my experiences. Maybe my stories will move you to write your stories. That's high achievement for a writing teacher. We would both benefit.

I

Growing Up, Taking Shape

1

my father's voice

remember my father calling my name on summer evenings when I was a boy in the late 1950s in northeastern Ohio. With neighborhood kids I played whiffle ball in the yard behind Doc Stires' office. Night fell fast, and sweat dried cold on the back of our necks. Stars appeared in the darkening sky. Lightning bugs pulsed a few feet off the ground. It was a magic time without daylight when a whiffle ball moved like a Whitey Ford fastball.

We had all promised to be home before dark, but no one was willing to break the spell. We played on with shouts and giddiness at the futility of catching and hitting in the growing dark. We must have known in our bones that there was something more important going on than the game. No one wanted to let it go. No one wanted to go home. Our play was summer and friendship and a tad of rebellion to be outside in the descending night beyond the time our parents wanted us home.

The first call came: my father's voice, short, booming, unmistakable, "Tom!"

My father's voice. No trace in it of an Italian accent. He had been in America since 1914 when he left Nola, a village near Naples, he then a child of nine.

My father's voice, still strong at fifty-four years old, calling from behind the screen door at the top of the fire escape on the porch of our apartment over his tavern and bowling alleys. He had owned those businesses since 1940. Throughout the 1920s and half of the 1930s he had worked in brickyards, taking the jobs his father and other Italian immigrants had been drawn to in Malvern, Ohio, and the surrounding towns.

My father's voice rising into the night sky, carrying over rooftops, alley, and neighbors' yards to land in my ears where I played with friends in the yard behind Doc Stires' office.

I ran all the way home—took twenty seconds, thirty tops. I reached the fire escape and looked up. My father's figure did not darken the screen door, but warm yellow light emanated from the apartment. He had worked hard to be successful in America. And like the Italian accent he had naturally left behind as a young learner of English, he also left behind much of his ethnicity.

There's a photograph in an oval frame of my father and two of his brothers taken soon after the family arrived in America: Giuseppe, Antonio, and Felice, my father, all dressed in soft caps with short bills, white shirts buttoned to the neck, belted waist coats, knickers, leggings, and sturdy leather shoes laced over their ankles. "Look," says the photo, a print of which was surely sent to relatives in Nola. "Look how well we are doing in America."

My father spoke Italian only occasionally, only to old Italian immigrants who had come to America in their late teens or twenties. Italian was the language they liked to speak. My father, however, liked to speak English. The old country was a distant memory for him that had little to do with the life he had made for himself. He'd become a United States citizen in 1936. He saw himself as an American businessman, not an Italian immigrant. I once asked an uncle of mine—Gigi Chiavari, my father's brother-in-law who lived to be ninety-three—why he had come to America when he was eighteen. "Why I come 'cross?" Uncle Gigi said. "Same reason everybody come 'cross. You make a better living, a better home, a better life."

That's what my father had done. I am fifty-nine years old now. It has been many years since I've heard my father's voice. But writing this, I hear it now: My father's voice at twilight on a summer evening in small-town America. My father's voice calling me home.

2

the place

I n one of my earliest memories I am on a barstool eating a boiled hot dog with my fingers. I don't need a bun, and the hot dog is so succulent I don't need ketchup. I must be five. It is morning and I wear pajamas. I'm not sitting, but rather kneeling atop the round, swiveling seat of a barstool. The seat is wobbly and covered with red vinyl. I like to twirl round and round on it, which makes me dizzy. The reason I am kneeling instead of sitting is so I will be high enough above the bar to reach the paper plate.

I'm in my dad's tavern—or beerjoint, as I called it. The year is 1954, and I am working on that hot dog at the back bar across from the kitchen area. Customers are few this early in the morning, but old Bill Hawkins stands at the end of the bar, wearing a white T-shirt, sipping a short draft beer. He had been one of two part-time police officers in town, a good one. Behind the bar, against the wall, is the steam table, where buns are kept soft and warm and where hot dogs slowly cook throughout the day in a water-filled stainless steel container. Another container is filled with Red's famous Coney Island sauce to spread over the hot dogs—a recipe of tomato sauce, hamburger, chopped onions, and spices. Next to the steam table is a large, flat grill that can hold thirty hamburgers at once if needed. I saw that happen one Friday night when the high school football team came in after a tough loss. Such sizzling and aroma among the subdued players! Next to the grill is an old refrigerator. In it are uncooked hot dogs, large jars of sliced dill pickles, mustard, and ketchup, loaves of salami, ham, goose liver, and cheese, both Swiss and American. Hamburger patties stacked and separated by layers of waxed paper await the lunch hour.

Next to the refrigerator, running up to the front of the tavern, is the back bar. Above it is a long mirror. Daddy (and I do call this long-ago Italian immigrant *Daddy*) can ring up a sale on the cash register, glance to the mirror, and see customers behind him. When the place is closed from 2:30 A.M. until 8:00 A.M., Daddy leaves the cash register drawer open with fifty dollars in the till. That's so any burglar won't destroy the expensive cash register during a theft. We were robbed several times when I was a child. High excitement with crashing doors, fleeing crooks, and once even a police officer's accidental gunshot that petrified one burglar hiding in the women's bathroom. On either side of the cash register are glass shelves holding scores of bottles of booze. On the bottom shelves are cheap whiskeys like Corby's and Kessler's. On the top shelves are more expensive whiskeys like Crown Royal, Seagram Seven, and various bourbons and scotches.

Technically, Daddy's business is a nightclub. The population of my hometown was so small that the state of Ohio allowed only two liquor licenses within the village corporation limits. My dad would have bought the cheaper five-hundred dollar license, but it had been purchased by his friend, Charlie Petrucci, who operated The Malvern Grill and Recreation. Daddy had to buy the nightclub license, which cost one thousand dollars per year. The only practical difference between the licenses was that Daddy could stay open until 2:30 A.M., which he always did. Charlie Petrucci had to close at 1:00 A.M. Outside, above the sidewalk hung a neon sign that intermittently flashed, "Red's Nite Club . . . Red's Nite Club . . . Red's Nite Club." Red was the name my dad went by, a reference to his auburn hair that had turned salt and pepper by the time I came along when he was forty-four. One of his brothers, Tony, and one sister, Filomina (Aunt Filmen) still had red hair.

My mother described Red's Nite Club as a working man's bar. Daddy had built it in 1940. Most customers were men who worked in steel mills and factories in nearby Canton or locally in small businesses and brickyards. Throughout the first half of the twentieth century, the area boomed with brickyards. Men worked hard and got plenty of overtime at places like Number Seven, Big Four, and Metropolitan Brick. On Fridays, Daddy kept $1,500 on hand to cash paychecks, a convenient service he offered customers that also boosted business. Some

customers ran a tab all week that Daddy kept track of on a notepad
next to the cash register. On payday they settled up.

There was no jukebox in Red's Nite Club. No music, no dancing,
no mixed drinks, unless you called highballs and boilermakers mixed
drinks. "Red's" was strictly a beer-and-shot bar, though in a cabinet behind glass he kept pints and fifths of cheap sweet wine he sold to men
we knew as winos.

Below the bar were the beer and pop coolers, the sinks for cleaning glasses, and big cardboard boxes for emptying trash. Cigarette ashes
were dumped into an empty coffee can. One of my jobs was to empty
the cardboard boxes into a large, round metal container behind the
place and burn the trash in it.

The coolest thing behind the bar were the taps. There were three
of them. Two drew beer from barrels in the walk-in cooler in the cel-
lar. It was frigid in there. You could see your breath in that cooler. The
third tap, the middle one, was yellow. Pull that and you got the cold-
est water you'd ever drunk. I loved coming into the bar from kick-the-
can or baseball, my face flushed, my white T-shirt so sweaty it stuck

to my back. I'd grab a large beer glass, shove it under the spout, and pull the yellow tap. I drank that cold water straight down until the back of my throat ached.

On either side of the rear entrance of the bar were the restrooms: men's on the right, women's on the left. In the women's was a sink and toilet. In the men's was a sink, a toilet, and a urinal. Attached to the wall above the sinks were cloth towel dispensers to dry your hands. You pulled down on a section of towel and the previously used section rotated up into the dispenser. The bathrooms were cleaned once a week. The women's restroom was used so infrequently that sometimes, when I was a teenager and had begun cleaning the bar on Sunday mornings, I'd skip it. The men's restroom was disgusting. It smelled like sewage and should have been cleaned every day. Yellow dots of dried urine splattered the porcelain. The rubber mesh at the bottom of the urinal was often clogged with soggy cigarette butts. When business was slow, Daddy put me on guard and used the women's restroom.

I knew more adult men than any other kid in town: Joe Columbo, Minner Knotts, Girard Recchio, Mike Montella (who looked like comedian Lou Costello), Boots Leatherberry, Joe Nardo, Tony Mason, Rudy Reed, Kenny Totten, Frank Mack (who looked like Babe Ruth), Harry McMasters, Tippy Palmer, Dick Contini, Johnny Tokos, Jimmy McCort, Bill Burwell (who looked like New York Yankee manager Casey Stengal), T-Bone Hahn, P-Rock Jones, Chuck Crawford, Norm Burwell, Bill Hawkins, and Mort McKinney (the first atheist I ever met). No one from the Lutheran church that my mom sent my sister and me to frequented the bar, even though it served the best sandwiches in town—the Coney Islands were wildly popular. Some of the customers were veterans of World War II. Bill Burwell had even fought in The Battle for Belleau Wood in World War I, 1918, a time that seemed impossibly long ago. Most customers sought the camaraderie the bar offered. I knew them all by their first names. They called me Tommy. Years later, I realized that some of the customers were alcoholics. Bill Hawkins, for example, the customer standing at the end of the bar, sipping the short draft as I ate the hot dog, made his rounds to all the beerjoints in the vicinity every morning, drinking one beer in each, always leaving a last sip in the glass. He got a buzz on early and sustained it throughout the day.

The men, the beer and whiskey, the sandwiches, my father moving briskly behind the bar, wearing a long white apron tied around his stomach . . . that was Red's. Sometimes I called it "the beerjoint," sometimes "the bar." Usually, though, my family called it "the place." That was more accurate, for attached to the bar by a doorway was a two-lane bowling alley, which was open every evening from late August through early May, except Thanksgiving, Christmas, New Year's day, and Easter. It was also open Sunday afternoons.

The place was my home, just as much as our four-bedroom apartment above it. I learned to read in first grade, but some of the first words I recognized were brands of beer: Hamms, Blatz, Rolling Rock, Stroh's, Duquesne (my introduction to French!), Iron City, and "Hey Mabel, Black Label, Carling Black Label Beer" (I knew the commercial jingles, too). Those names appeared stamped on beer cases, labeled on bottles, and written in the glass of neon signs hanging in the window advertising brands of beer. Rudy Reed introduced me to the funnies in the *Cleveland Plain Dealer* that was delivered each morning. I became an avid reader of "The Phantom" and "Gil Thorp," the strip about a high school coach. I don't remember what Mr. Thorp taught. Sports, I guess.

I spent so much time in the place because Daddy put me to work. Work was the only respectable way, he figured. Work and some risk had taken him from Italy to the United States, from the brickyards to ownership of his own business. "I don't care if you become a ditch digger," he said, "just be a good ditch digger."

I burned the trash. I set pins in the bowling alley (no automatic pin setters in Red's). I'd earn eight cents a line, which figured out to sixteen dollars if I set two hundred of them—that amounted to about twenty-eight hours in the bowling ball pits lifting pins and sixteen-pound bowling balls. I graduated from setting pins to "watching" the alleys, which meant renting bowling shoes, collecting money, tabulating the lines the pin boys set, keeping score for novice bowlers until they caught on, recording the outcome of league games in the official book with a carbon copy for each team captain, and updating the chalkboard high on the wall that showed the league standings with each team's won/lost record. I painted the gutters and cleaned the ball pits, always amazed at how much dirt collected under the thick rubber mats.

I cleaned wooden bowling pins in the basement with steel wool (an awful job) then wiped them clean of grit and brushed on a coat of lacquer to protect them against the pounding. Sometimes when the bar was busy at lunch, I helped Daddy by frying hamburgers, making Coneys and sandwiches, getting bottles of pop for customers (the beer taps were off limits).

Following my freshmen year of high school, I began cleaning the place on Sundays. My main job was sweeping and mopping the linoleum floor, which meant beneath the booths along the wall and in and around the twenty barstools bolted to the floor. Every two weeks (or three or four if I could stretch it out), I did the job I tried to avoid. After sweeping and mopping, while the floor was drying, I hauled a five-gallon can of liquid wax from the basement, wrapped a soft cloth applicator around the head of the waxer, and screwed a slat into place to secure it.

Waxing the floors of the bar and bowling alley took an hour and fifteen minutes. I poured a pool of wax onto the linoleum, soaked the cloth applicator in it, then began applying wax, moving my arms to and fro, backing up a step or two as I worked. I never liked waxing the floor until I was doing it. Once I was doing it, I'd catch a rhythm of pouring and waxing, stepping back, waxing, stopping, pouring, working the wax evenly over the floor. The green linoleum of the bar and the red linoleum of the bowling alley shined as I spread the wax, rubbing out puddles that formed in tiny valleys where the linoleum was uneven.

I waxed around the base of each bar stool, small, tricky places where I couldn't pour wax or maneuver the applicator very well. This was tedious, but I worked deliberately, tilting the applicator on its side, using the edge to wax the floor around the base of each stool. I worked all the way down the length of the bar, bending to the task, the minutes passing quickly. The wax darkened the floor, drying to a gloss that reflected morning light passing through the glass door and large window.

When I finished, I straightened up and pressed my fingers to the small of my back. I leaned the handle of the wax applicator against the bar and reached my arms high above my head. I could feel the pleasurable stretching of muscles in my shoulders, back, and arms. I always finished the job by waxing the floor behind the bar. I took the can of wax and stored it in the basement. At the washtub I removed the applicator, no longer fluffy and clean, and held it under warm running water. I squeezed out as much water and wax as I could, then set the applicator on the edge of the washtub to dry.

By this time, the area I'd waxed first by the front door had dried. Before I left the bar, I looked over my work. Sometimes I'd see a dull patch of linoleum I had missed, often around one of the barstools. I retrieved a bar towel, knelt by the part of the floor I had finished last and dabbed the towel in wet wax. I went to the spot I had missed, knelt again, and rubbed the towel over it until the surface shined darkly.

I threw the towel into the cardboard laundry box at the top of the basement steps and walked to the front door, brushing my hands on my Levis. I looked back over my work once more. The floor was impeccably clean, shining, protected by a coat of wax. By Wednesday the floor would look dull. It didn't look that way now, and now was what mattered. The good ditch digger had done his work.

3

neighbors

The Thompsons lived behind my dad's tavern until just before school started in 1956. They had been part of my life since my birth. I knew the parents as Mr. Thompson and Mrs. Thompson. They had six children, though the two oldest, T. L. and Nail, were grown and gone, both having joined the armed service. Doris, Jack, Billy, and Joey were the children I knew well. Doris was like a second mother in the family. Once when Billy, Joey, and I got shut inside a shed, she hearkened to our cries and rescued us by unsticking the door. Jack was my sister's age, nine years older than I. He'd taught me to ride a two-wheeler, walking and trotting behind me as I pedaled down the sidewalk, his hand on and off the bicycle seat, steadying me when needed. Billy showed me how to fight and defend myself from a neighborhood bully. Joey, just one year older than I, was my best friend. Every Thompson family member knew what I'd say when I came to their door: "Can Joey come out to play?"

The house the Thompsons lived in was two stories and had just four rooms. You walked in the front door to the kitchen, where they ate meals and Mrs. Thompson washed clothes in an old ringer washing machine she stored in a closet without a door. Next to the kitchen was a room with a couch, chairs, and a television. A coal stove there heated the entire house, including the two bedrooms upstairs. No laundry room. No guest bedroom. No recreation room. No bathroom.

Life was elemental and frugal at the Thompsons. Joey wore clothing handed down from Billy. Mrs. Thompson hung laundry outside on a line or sometimes on a line rigged up zigzagging across the kitchen. Keeping warm was a priority. Whenever I visited during cold weather, the family was gathered in the room made toasty by the coal stove.

I backed into that coal stove once and came home with a scorched coat.

The Thompsons were closer to their food, too. Some Sundays I watched the brothers in the front yard take turns wringing the neck of a live chicken, a wild scene in which the chicken was throttled by grabbing its throat and squeezing while swinging it round and round. The chicken didn't go quietly into that good night. It squawked and beat its wings furiously, filling the air with feathers. Mrs. Thompson soaked the chicken carcass in a metal tub of boiling water so she could pluck feathers more easily.

Every now and then some of the family and Mr. Thompson took cane fishing poles to a lake or creek and returned hours later with a mess of blue gill. One summer afternoon as I sat on the low cement porch of their house with my feet in the dirt and my elbows on my knees, Mrs. Thompson came out of the kitchen in her apron and handed me a piece of crispy fried blue gill and a flaky, homemade biscuit still warm from the oven.

One snowy winter day when I was five or six years old, I went outside to build a snowman. Mom dressed me in a new red snowsuit—a bulky coat with matching leggings that gave my gait a robotic quality. The gravel parking area behind the place wasn't good for playing since beer trucks and customers were always pulling in to park temporarily. Joey's yard, however, was perfect. The dirt and stones were covered with six inches of snow that hadn't been tramped down. From my back steps at the bottom of the fire escape, I trudged past the Thompsons' two sheds near our property. One shed was a bin where the family retrieved chunks of coal for the stove. The other was a two-seat outhouse. Sunlight filtered through the boards and the roof. I couldn't resist looking into the holes now and then to see the mixture of toilet paper and glistening shit. I feared falling in, imagined this every time Joey held on to the seat so his skinny butt wouldn't drop through the hole. On hot days I held my breath and ran past the outhouse into the neighborhood.

This winter day, though, snow fell hard and most everything was frozen and scentless. I stepped onto the low porch of the Thompson house, stamped my boots on the cement, and crossed to knock on the door. I heard movement inside.

The door opened just enough for Doris to peek through. She saw me and opened wider. "Tommy Romano, what you doing out on a day like this?"

"Can Joey come out to play?"

"Too cold and too much snow, but you ask him." Doris turned her head and called over her shoulder, "Joey!"

A moment later Joey's head popped by his sister's waist. It looked like a brown balloon with close cropped hair and wide eyes.

"Can you come out?" I asked. Joey looked beyond me to the snow falling in the yard, on the fire escape, on the roof of the outhouse.

"Man," he said, "you must be crazy."

"We'll build a snowman," I said.

Joey squinted and wrinkled his nose. He looked at me, he looked at the snow.

"You got to decide, Joey," Doris said. "I ain't leaving this door open all day."

Joey shrugged his shoulders. "OK." He disappeared and Doris shut the door.

I turned to the falling snow, packed a snowball, and began rolling. I got the ball as big as I could and rolled it with all my might to the middle of the yard. The snow was falling so hard you'd think it would make noise, but it didn't. It was soundless. Still no Joey. I went back to the door, knocked again, waited. The door opened a crack, then farther.

"Hey," I said, "you comin'?"

The warmth from the coal stove wafted against my face. I touched a mitten to my red cheek. Joey was a sprite, barefoot, wearing a faded sweatshirt misshapen around the neck. He raised his lip and smoke curled out of his mouth.

"Where'd you get that?"

Joey blew more smoke through the screen door.

I could do that. I huffed out foggy breath from deep in my lungs, then asked again, "Where'd you get your smoke?"

Joey grinned. "I'll be out in a minute." He closed the door. I went back to building the snowman.

Joey never came outside that day. At one of my knocks, he invited me in. I took off my boots and snowsuit in the kitchen and joined the Thompsons in the room with the coal stove. They watched a fuzzy black-and-white picture on television, the rabbit ears skewed just right to get even that good of a picture.

Joey went over to his mother who sat on the end of the couch. Mrs. Thompson's right hand rested on her knee, a cigarette held between her fingers. Joey leaned over and attached his mouth to the cigarette. He sucked in. The end of the cigarette flared orange. He turned to me and let smoke slip out the corners of his mouth, blinking as it moved past his eyes.

Joey knew many things I did not, and, as the youngest of six children, he had experienced far more than I had. I looked upon him as an older, wiser brother. Through Joey and his brother, Billy, I learned words that were useful in arguments, words I knew not to let my mother hear me say. When Joey's female cousins visited, we kids got under a tarp that covered a stack of building bricks. There I learned that girls and boys were different in significant ways.

One summer afternoon I got into a pitched verbal battle over some trifle with the neighborhood kids. Fearing for my safety, I fled up the fire escape to our porch and quickly latched the screen door. The kids

jeered and shouted at me from the gravel parking area. I got to my knees on the glider, so I could see through the screen and jeer and shout back.

The arguing went on awhile. I was red-faced and righteous. I knew I had been wronged. I let the neighbor kids know it, using some of those new words I'd learned. During the shouting, I heard the door to our apartment open. I was mortified, but it wasn't my mom, wielding the yardstick and a bar of soap. It was Joey. He said nothing but looked smug. He had gone around to the front of the building, climbed the stairs, knocked on the front door, and asked my mother if he could join me on the back porch. She let him into the apartment, and he made his way down the hallway to the back door. When I turned from my perch on the glider to see Joey step nonchalantly onto the porch, I was stunned and speechless. Joey glanced my way, but said nothing. He walked to the screen door, unlatched it, and descended the fire escape to join the kids.

I was relieved to know that I wasn't going to get beat up. I like to think Joey knew that I, his friend, was acting spoiled and unreasonable, and that he was patiently showing me I wasn't so all-fired safe on the porch, and I'd be wise to end this nonsense immediately. Even at six or seven years old, Joey was cool-headed and diplomatic. He was small and smart. Around adults he was quiet and bashful. With me he was talkative, even instructive.

More than fifty years later, I'm still in touch with Joey. We live at opposite ends of Ohio, but every now and then one of us will make contact. One time when we hadn't communicated in years, I telephoned him. When he answered, I said, "Can Joey come out to play?"

"Is this Tommy Romano?" he said, laughing. "Man, I'll break your thumbs!"

The day in 1956 when the Thompsons moved to Canton was a sad one. Furniture and boxes filled that yard of stones and dirt, waiting to be packed into the bed of a truck. Joey stood in the dirt a few feet from an upright, freestanding mirror. He was crying. Somehow the mirror had been cracked. Mr. Thompson blamed Joey for throwing a stone that did the damage. That's the only time I ever remember Mr. Thompson angry, and stressed, too, I imagine, on this day of the move after ten years in the same house. He shouted. My best friend cried, tears filling his eyes, streaking his cheeks, his nose running.

"You know, Tommy," Joey told me not long ago, "my dad said that before we left Malvern, Mr. Red offered to give him the money to build a bathroom inside the house."

I hadn't known that. I felt a little cynical in questioning my father's motives. Did he really want the Thompsons to stay or did he just want to remove once and for all the stench of the outhouse behind the tavern and apartment?

No one ever moved into the Thompsons' vacant house. The sheds were torn down immediately, the outhouse hole filled in. I sometimes got into the house through a window and explored. It was dreadful. Windows were broken. Linoleum in the kitchen was curling. The bedroom floors upstairs were made of rough wood. It was hard to believe that Mr. and Mrs. Thompson and the children had lived in just four rooms, only two of them bedrooms. In one of them, Mrs. Thompson and Doris slept in one bed, Mr. Thompson in another. In the second bedroom, Jack, Billy, and Joey slept.

As dreadful as the empty house was, the Thompsons had made it a home full of warmth and bodies and noise and the good smells of Mrs. Thompson's cooking. Now it was just a musty, dilapidated shell, built cheaply, worn out, trashy and unfit for human habitation. In a few years, the house was demolished, the debris removed, and the lot graveled over to make for parking.

As a teenager I came to understand that the Thompsons' move to Canton was a good one. The family rented a house with indoor plumbing and heating. Mr. Thompson got better work. Joey ended up going to Timken High School. Canton was a city, not a village. The black community was large. Intellectually, I understood why my best childhood friend had to leave.

Still, I wish the Thompsons hadn't moved. I wish Mr. Thompson had taken my father's offer to pay for an indoor bathroom. As children, I once told Billy and Joey that I wanted us to live together when we grew up. We'd have a house, more like my house than theirs. We'd have food like their mother made. We'd have toys and play all day. We'd go fishing and beat up anybody in the neighborhood who caused trouble. Best of all, we'd have a big neon sign over our front door, just like my dad's neon sign in front of the place. In fancy handwriting our sign would read,

Billy, Joey, and Tommy

It would blink on and off all day long to show everyone where the three best buddies in the world lived.

That was a delightful child fantasy, born out of my affection for Billy and Joey and my unique experience growing up with my dad owning a bar business. I know my wish that the Thompsons hadn't moved was about my own selfishness. My reality was growing up in a white family whose income was upper, middle class. That wasn't the Thompsons' reality. They were black in a largely white, largely segregated community. The Thompsons lived in the center of our small town in substandard housing. There weren't many outhouses still in use in Malvern by the mid-1950s. It figures that one of them would be for a house rented to a black family.

I think I would have grown up to be a better kid, a better teenager, a better man, had Joey and I remained friends with near daily contact. He was a year ahead of me. We could have walked to school each

morning. He could have taught me the ins-and-outs of each grade. He could have kept me grounded with his playfulness and skills of diplomacy, with the way he instructed quietly with words. The key word here is *proximity*, the opposite of "out of sight, out of mind." Daily contact with Joey and the Thompsons, the only black family living smack in the middle of town, not in a settlement at the edge of the corporation limit, would have kept me aware of another America, one that my fast friend inhabited, another America that was easily forgotten as I became an adolescent and made a subtle and inexorable move myself into an America split by race.

4

home office

I set up my first home office when I was fifteen. My parents were remodeling our spacious, four-bedroom living quarters above the place, converting our apartment into two so that we could rent one. The major work was creating a new, eat-in kitchen out of what had been the dining room. The work was nearly complete but with no renter yet, we were still using the entire apartment.

I commandeered the breakfast nook in the back kitchen. Miss Ayers—who had taught my uncle Charlie twenty-five years earlier—required all freshmen to write a book report that spring. In the one-room library attached to the study hall, I had found a gem of a book—a new juvenile biography of Jack Dempsey, the heavyweight-boxing champion from 1919 to 1926. I knew about Dempsey from articles in boxing magazines and from a piece he had written for *The Readers' Digest*. Even forty years after he had been champion, the name *Dempsey* was in the air in my dad's blue-collar bar, where sports was a mainstay of conversation. There was also this: my half-brother, Jack Nigro, whose father had been a boxer in the 1930s, was named after Dempsey—not John, not Jonathan, but Jack.

The book consumed me. I was ripe for a good story about boxing. I had been a big fan of Floyd Patterson, the first heavyweight champion to lose and then regain the title. I was also fascinated by Muhammad Ali, then going by his given name that I had never heard the like of: Cassius Marcellus Clay. In boxing magazines, I learned about his brashness, color, and playful personality. He wrote and proclaimed his own poetry, touting his greatness and predicting the rounds in which he would knock out opponents. A man reciting poetry? An athlete, no less? A professional boxer? Most athletes I knew about in the 1950s and early 1960s were modest, reserved, and uncontroversial. Their accomplishments spoke for themselves. And they certainly didn't write poetry. . . .

. . . Like Jack Dempsey of the "roaring twenties." He had been a tiger in the ring, lean, mauling, and vicious. His fights often ended in the early rounds with Dempsey destroying opponents in a furious on-slaught of punches. Like many boys, I was drawn to violence and may-hem. Dempsey's fights were incredible. On one occasion, he was actually brawled through the ropes, out of the ring, and onto the type-writers of the press sitting below the ring apron. A reporter pushed him back into the ring and Dempsey went on to knock out his Argentinean opponent, Luis Angel Firpo, the "wild bull of the Pampas." Wild bull of the pampas? In fourth grade geography I'd learned what the pam-pas was, but I'd never thought about what a man would be like as a wild bull on it. The language and metaphor fired my imagination. I learned how Dempsey—after a three-year layoff from boxing—had lost the title to Gene Tunney, a literature loving, ex-marine, who had beaten the champ with sharp boxing skills that kept Dempsey off balance and adroit footwork that kept Tunney away from Dempsey's dogged pur-suit. I learned how Dempsey knocked Tunney down in the rematch with a combination of powerful punches and how Tunney recovered during the infamous "long count" that gave him as many as fourteen seconds to recover his senses, get back on his feet, survive the round, and go on to beat Dempsey in a decision.

This was great stuff to my male, adolescent mind. The biography had it all: a rise from poverty and obscurity, strength and heroism, tri-umph and defeat, bravery and foolishness, victory almost gained then lost through confusion and controversy.

My study hall teacher approved of my reading. That was Mr. Turk, the burly industrial arts teacher and assistant football coach. He stood by my desk, his thick arms crossed on his chest, leaned forward, and squinted to see the book I was reading. "Ah, Dempsey, now there was a fighter," said Mr. Turk. "You know, he soaked his face in pickle brine to toughen his skin so he wouldn't cut. You come to that part yet?"

I shook my head.

"What a champ. He'd mop the floor with Clay."

I wasn't so sure about that. Two months earlier, I'd won a dollar by betting that Cassius Clay would beat Sonny Liston. My buddies and the men in my father's bar all thought I was foolish, but I had faith in the poet. I also had faith in his six-foot-three-inch height, 210 pounds, and flashing speed of fist and foot.

My book report for Miss Ayers was going to be first-rate. But I needed a place to work. There was no desk in our apartment, so I set up everything I needed on the table of the breakfast nook, a booth of sorts built into the wall of the back kitchen. Since my mom, dad, and I were eating meals in the new kitchen, the breakfast nook went unused. I used it.

My sister had bequeathed me her manual typewriter, a portable Royal that she had named "Pete," printing the name in red nail polish on its side. I set Pete in the middle of the table and placed everything I needed nearby: a tablet of typing paper, pens of different colored ink, pencils, an ink eraser that kind of worked if I was patient and careful and didn't tear the paper, the Dempsey bio, and my report that I had written during study hall in my unremarkable handwriting.

I had no typing skills. The organization of the keyboard made no sense. The work was laborious with me hunting out each letter and punching the appropriate key. It took me ten seconds to type *D e m p s e y*, provided I didn't make a mistake, a common occurrence. I routinely forgot to activate the shift bar to make capital letters. Roll up the baton a little, apply the ink eraser, gently, brush away the eraser crumbs, roll down the baton, press the shift key and type the capital letter.

But what a transformation! My tilted, pedestrian handwriting squeezed between the blue lines of ragged-edged paper torn from my College Student Composition Book became, right before my eyes, printed words, just as you saw in books. I wasn't just typing a report. I was becoming an author! My words were becoming like Cassius Clay's poems in the boxing magazines. Over a period of days, I spent time each evening pecking out letters. As I worked, I sometimes saw that the text I'd handwritten fell short in some way. Maybe I had left out words or composed something that didn't make sense upon rereading. Sometimes what I had written didn't match my strong feelings about the book, particularly when I was retelling Dempsey's important fights. When that happened, I stopped typing and paged through the book, browsing, rereading, rethinking.

Then I diligently plagiarized scenes, mixing in some of my language with the author's exciting wording. I didn't suspect that I was doing anything wrong, wouldn't even learn of the word *plagiarism* until I began teaching. I just wanted to capture for Miss Ayers the excitement I felt about the book, about boxing, about Dempsey. The author told his story so well it was impossible for me not to borrow from him. I would do what he had done: use words to communicate compelling events.

My report contained no criticism, judgment, or evaluation. I was just driven to retell the story of this larger-than-life character. Dempsey was my Odysseus, and I was a kind of Homer, telling of the boxer's exploits and overlooking his flaws, much as the writer of the juvenile biography had done. I worked hard and steady on the report, putting in my time, making workmanlike progress, realizing my accomplishment all along the way. I'd type a page number at the bottom of a sheet of paper, then wind it out of the carriage, and lay it on the modest pile of typed pages. I rolled a new sheet into the carriage, double-checked where I had left off, then began hunting and punching, erasing errors, rereading, adding new sentences, becoming a writer. It was satisfying work, way better than setting pins or burning the trash.

5

phone call

~~~~~

May 8, 1964. I am fifteen years old, a ninth grader. A Friday night. Only three weeks of school left. The weather surprisingly warm in northeastern Ohio this evening. I am giddy with the imminent end of school, the blessed weekend just begun, and the warm weather that means excellent playing conditions for our high school baseball team. My dad is away for the night at a bowling tournament in nearby Canton, Ohio. He formed a team with four of his customers and drove them to Canton in his new Cadillac.

I'm up late on this weekend night, watching television, as is my wont. Mom has been in bed awhile. The show I try not to miss on Friday nights at 11:20 is Channel 8's "Shock Theater," horror hosted by the outrageous Ghoulardi (i.e., Ernie Anderson). I'd already watched Vincent Price in *The Bat*. Now I am watching Spencer Tracy in *Northwest Passage*.

Sometime deep into the movie the telephone rings. I leap from the lounge chair and run to the kitchen to answer it before the ringing wakens my mother.

I pick up the receiver. A woman's voice says, "Is this the residence of Philip Romano?"

"Yes," I answer. Immediately I sense something wrong.

A pause. I hear scratching and rubbing, like the caller is holding the mouthpiece of the telephone against her clothing.

The voice again: "Is this one of the Romano boys?"

Something is not right. I am the only Romano boy, the only son of my father and mother. Still, my father has six brothers. Maybe that's what's confusing the caller. "Yes," I say. "I'm one of the Romano boys."

Another pause, longer this time, more scratching, rubbing, and muffled voices. I listen intently. There seems to be a question and answering going on. A creeping dread makes me swallow. I feel that dropping sensation in the bowels.

"This is the emergency room of the Alliance City Hospital," says the voice, "and we have Philip Romano here and he's dead."

6

surrealism

have a greeting card a friend sent to me that I've saved for years. On its front cover is a man sitting at a desk in a classroom, taking a test. His expression is startled. Your eyes follow his gaze to the lower right of the frame: on the floor an ink pen, smiling broadly, pencil-thin arms and legs pumping, flees from the desk. The caption reads, "While answering a question on surrealism his pen ran out."

I encountered the concept of surrealism only after I'd begun teaching. My students and I were reading William Faulkner's compelling short story, "Barn Burning." I found a filmstrip that explained the concept of surrealism, that literary and artistic movement that sought to depict the workings of the unconscious mind, those irrational dreamlike states that seemed a super reality. The filmstrip looped through a series of fantastical images by Salvador Dali and other surrealist painters, while voices explained the elements of surrealism and read passages from Faulkner whose images were equally fantastic, whose language expanded time and described action occurring in dreamlike states that strained readers' ability to perceive them.

At fifteen years old I did not have the word, but surrealism is what I experienced in the minutes and hours after I learned of my father's death.

"You'll have to talk to my mother," I said to the voice on the telephone. I set down the receiver and ran to my parents' bedroom. I took Mom's shoulder, shook her roughly, rousing her from deep sleep, shouting, "Mom! Mom! The phone! Answer the phone."

Mom reeled to waking, disoriented, confused. "What, Tommy? What?"

I wouldn't say, couldn't say. "Get the phone!" I shouted. I wanted her to go to the kitchen, pick up the telephone receiver, listen, talk, then tell me that what I knew was true was not.

Mom swept the sheet aside. She moved with urgency. My hysteria had frightened her. Her eyes were wide, her hair disheveled. I followed her to the telephone. She picked it up, said something, waited, then screamed, wailed, threw her head back and her arms toward the ceiling as though she'd been hit in the chest by a shotgun blast. Freed, the telephone receiver rose into the air, tumbling and turning, rising as high as the cord would permit, then falling. In all these years it has not landed. It is tumbling still.

My mind was a blank from that point until sometime later when I remember sitting on the couch. Mom sat between my sister and me. We held her in our arms. Relatives arrived, my father's brothers and sisters, their families, my mother's brothers and sisters. Mom and Nancy and I wept. We were inconsolable. "If there was only more time," my mother said. "If there was only more time."

She was worried, terrified, I learned later, about the overwhelming responsibility she suddenly faced. She knew nothing about running the business end of the tavern and bowling alleys. She could tend bar, was savvy about customer relations, knew how to clean, but in all the years they'd been married, Daddy had shown her nothing about keeping the books, paying taxes, ordering supplies, or maintaining the bowling alleys. "If there was only more time," she said. "Red could have taught me. If there was only more time."

In the midst of writing this chapter, I called my sister. In forty-three years I had never talked to her about the particulars of how she had experienced that night. She was twenty-four, the mother of a four-year-old boy from her first marriage. She had remarried the fall of that year, was pregnant with her second child.

"Did Mom call you first that night?" I asked. "I don't remember anything between the time Mom reacted to the call and later when we sat on the couch, all the relatives in the apartment."

"She must have," Nancy said, "but I didn't answer the phone. Rodger did. I was asleep. He must have closed the place and just gotten home. Remember, we lived in the orange brick house up by

Howard Schreiber's." I could sense her reconstructing the memory as she talked.

"He woke me," said Nancy. "There were tears in his eyes. He said, 'It's your dad. There's been a wreck. We have to go.' Then he gathered Philip in a blanket, and we left."

Philip was the four-year-old, my nephew. After her divorce, he and Nancy had lived with us. Philip was like my little brother.

"When I got to the apartment, Mom was sitting on the couch," Nancy said. "You were in your bedroom. Do you remember that?"

I didn't. And then Nancy told me things that explained the hole I'd had in that night for forty-three years:

"There was no light on in your room," she said, "but I could see you from the kitchen light. You were on your side, facing the wall, curled up in that fetal position.

"I said, 'Are you all right, Tommy?' You said, 'No.' I said, 'Do you want Philip to sleep with you a little bit?' You said, 'Yes.'"

So my sister laid her son beside me. A four-year-old at three in the morning, slumbering heavily.

"Who called the relatives?" I asked.

"It must have been Rodger. I was sitting with Mom. I told her that maybe it was a mistake. Rodger went to Alliance to identify the body. I told mom we'd only know for sure when he got back."

That information jogged my memory: "Did Uncle Jimmy go to Alliance with him?"

"I believe so," said Nancy.

I remember my sister-in-law, Mary Ann, as an angel that dreadful night. She was married to my half-brother, Jack. I remember rising from the couch to my feet. It must have been near dawn. Mary Ann walked beside me, her right hand holding my elbow, her left arm around my back, her hand pressing my waist, holding me close. I moved in slow motion, not walking really, but floating, moving fluidly, weightless, ghostlike. We moved through the blurry shapes of aunts and uncles and cousins. One face suddenly loomed close, off to the right. It was round and unshaven, my cousin, Joey Chiavari, whom Mom always had me call Uncle Joey, since he was almost twenty years older than I. Uncle Joey's dark hair lay on his forehead. His broken eyes searched mine. Then his face receded as we moved through the kitchen toward my bedroom door.

Suddenly I wasn't floating anymore. I was sitting on the edge of the bed. A hand flat on my chest pressed me back to the pillow. My cotton blanket swished over me and floated down. Sleep found me, exhausted and trapped. My mind finally shut down awhile, left the surreal nightmare of reality.

I awoke to a dream in my head: My father sat on a cot in a prison cell. He leaned forward, elbows on his knees, wringing his hands. "If there was only more time," he said. "If there was only more time."

7

argument

~~~~~~

A few days before he was killed, my father and I had a vicious argument. I thought he was controlling and pig-headed, so concerned about his business that whatever I wanted was of no consequence.

The bowling season had ended, and as much as I loved to bowl, season's end meant I was free. Since the beginning of September, every Monday, Tuesday, and Wednesday night from 6:45 until 11:15 or 11:30 I tended the cash register in the bowling alley and made sure that everything went smoothly. But after the season ended, Daddy wanted me to hang around the bar. He had purchased an Arcade Bowling Machine that he fit along the wall near the massive air conditioner.

The bowling machine featured an alley about fifteen feet long. Players rolled miniature bowling balls at plastic bowling pins elevated a little above the alley and attached to the machine at the top. The ball didn't actually strike the pins. There were little steel triggers on the alley. When the ball struck those, bowling pins flipped backward and up. Just as in a regular bowling alley, the ball was picked up from a ball pit and rolled back to the bowler on an incline. An electronic board kept score. You could roll a game by yourself or form teams and compete with as many as three on a side.

Team competition was what my father had in mind. He envisioned many of the bowlers from the leagues that had just ended continuing to bowl using the machine. He'd make money from the dime a game it cost each player to bowl, plus the money they spent for beer, pop, chips, pretzels, and Coneys. My mom always said that Daddy was a real "promoter." He was good at getting people—mainly men—to participate in bowling leagues, golf leagues, and card games. He wasn't, however, sure that the bowling game would catch on, so he wanted me to hang around, just in case someone needed a partner.

I was simmering, sullen, and brooding. I was fifteen, in the last weeks of my freshman year of high school. I didn't want to hang around the bar on these mild spring evenings, bowling on a machine with my dad's customers who were ten, twenty, and thirty years older than I. I wanted to go out with my friends.

Dad's scheme failed miserably. No one showed up to launch league play on the bowling machine, so there I was, biding my time, imagining what my friends were doing, looking repeatedly at the clock on the wall. As the minutes ticked by, my simmer turned to a boil.

At eight o'clock I went to Daddy by the back bar where he cleaned beer glasses, dunking them in soapy water and plunging them over the upright brushes.

"Can I go now?" It was not a question. I said it as an ultimatum, with considerable bitterness and a tone that I hoped communicated, "What a fool you are!"

Daddy glanced at the clock. "Half an hour more."

"No one's coming!"

"They might. Some were interested."

"Do you see them?" I swept my hand back toward the bowling machine.

"Half an hour," he said, then turned, wiping his hands on a bar towel, patting them dry on the front of the long, white bartender's apron he wore.

At eight-thirty I slipped on my jacket and stomped out of the bar. I didn't ask permission. I didn't look my father's way. Once on the sidewalk, I bubbled over, spewing every curse word I knew that might apply to my money-grubbing dad.

That son-of-a-bitch, I thought. That heartless bastard.

We didn't say much to each other the entire week. I was resentful and sulking. Dad wasn't apologizing.

Later in the week, I softened. I began to feel guilty for the way I had acted. That Friday night, as Dad was walking down the hallway toward the back door to go down the steps of the fire escape to leave for the bowling tournament, I caught up with him from behind, walked at his side, touched the elbow of his brown cardigan sweater, the elbow that had pained him all winter, the one he'd have injected every now and then with cortisone so he could bowl.

"Roll a 600 tonight," I said.

I can't remember if he replied. Seems like he shrugged, maybe mumbled something like, "We'll see." If he'd forgiven my insolence from earlier in the week, I couldn't tell. He didn't turn his eyes on me. He seemed to have his mind on other things. Maybe the upcoming bowling match. Maybe the drive to Canton. Maybe how he could get that bowling machine league off the ground. Maybe plagues on his mind that I couldn't even imagine. But I had reached out to him, and for that I am ever grateful. He couldn't have mistaken my gesture. I'd spoken positive, upbeat words, wishing him success. I'd touched him, on this, the last night of his life.

8

solace

Hunt, punch. Hunt, punch. Dempsey wins the title in 1919 against Jess Willard, knocks him down seven times in the first round. Willard is six inches taller and sixty pounds heavier. Dempsey annihilates him. Hunt, punch. Hunt, punch. Four years later in a title fight against Luis Angel Firpo, Dempsey is knocked out of the ring, but climbs back in to knock out Firpo. Hunt, punch. Hunt, punch. After a three-year layoff, Dempsey fights Gene Tunney and loses the title. Tunney isn't a strong puncher but he is a masterful boxer. His ring generalship, I learn, is superb. Hunt, punch. Hunt, punch. Dempsey fights Jack Sharkey to earn a rematch with Tunney. When Sharkey turns his head to complain to the referee about a low blow, Dempsey knocks him out. Hunt, punch. Hunt, punch. In the championship rematch, Dempsey finally catches Tunney in the seventh round against the ropes, lands a combination of powerful punches. Tunney crumples to the canvas. Dempsey fails to go to a neutral corner. The referee does not start counting until he does so. Tunney gets as many as fourteen seconds to recover. He survives the round. Dempsey never catches him again, even stops his pursuit at one point and motions Tunney to come on and fight. Tunney keeps dancing and boxing and retains his title with a convincing decision over Dempsey. Hunt, punch. Hunt, punch.

This work hunched over the manual typewriter in the breakfast nook was not surreal. It was as purposeful and absorbing as sweeping, mopping, and waxing the floor in the place.

Two days after my father's death, we—the immediate family—went to Deckman's Funeral Home to view the body. There was my father, lying in the casket. He wore a suit, his face in a perpetual frown, his hands resting on his stomach, a rosary of black beads clutched in his right fist. Even though my sister and I hadn't been raised Catholic, all the relatives on my dad's side of the family were Catholic. I knew the rosary had religious significance. And I knew my dad's clutching it was wrong. I'd never known him to go to church. He'd never spoken of God's love or eternity or salvation. The only times, in fact, I'd ever heard him speak the names of God or Jesus were when he cursed. During visitation, I overheard someone ask Uncle Charlie if my dad had been religious. Uncle Charlie was devoutly Catholic. He had been crippled from polio since he was a baby. "Red wasn't religious," said Uncle Charlie. "He left the church as a boy, just stopped going." So the rosary my dad clutched, I knew, was not right.

In addition to that special viewing, we visited the funeral home four more times. On Monday, there were morning, afternoon, and evening visitations. On Tuesday morning, there was a prayer service. (Even though Daddy had been baptized Catholic, his funeral could not be held in the Catholic church, because he had married my mother, a non-Catholic. Seven years earlier when he had been in the hospital in critical condition from a massive heart attack, he had been told by Father Wiggins that he could be given the last rites of the Church if he renounced his marriage to my mother. Daddy had spurned the offer.)

Hundreds visited the funeral home. My father had eight siblings, my mother seven. I had scores of cousins. These numbers, however, were dwarfed by the hundreds of friends and customers from thirty years in business.

Even though I was fifteen, this was the first funeral and calling hours I'd ever attended. So many flowers loaded the tables and floor that to this day, whenever I come upon the strong sent of flowers, I'm reminded of those agonizing four days.

My mother and sister and I sat in front of the coffin. People passed by, an endless stream, it seemed, and they all stopped to offer their condolences. One young customer of my dad's, a man I'd known for years, grasped my shoulder and said, "Be strong, Tommy." Lawrence Faccini, an old Italian immigrant and family friend who had lost a teenage son in an electrical accident a few years earlier, genuflected over my father's body. A girl I liked at school came with her brother to pay their respects. My heart sped up when I saw her. I was ashamed that I could even think in that way when my father lay dead in front of me. At one point my mother, sister, and I knelt beside the coffin and said the Lord's Prayer. I sobbed so hard I could barely speak the words. I clasped my hands, pressing them hard against my forehead.

Thy kingdom come.

Tears burned the skin slick between my fingers.

Thy will be done.

My father, clean-shaven with makeup, frowning forever, dead in a coffin. Was this God's will?

Forever and ever.

When my mom and sister and I were leaving the funeral home, before I stepped through the doorway out of the room, I looked back to see my dad's brother Giuseppe, the oldest of the nine Romano children, approach the casket. The funeral director stood in his path. My uncle muscled him aside, leaned into the coffin, his head disappearing. I heard three brutal kisses—smack, smack, smack.

Amen.

Over those four days—Saturday through Tuesday—relatives and friends came and went to our apartment. They wanted to be with us, to tell us how sorry they were. They wanted to be around these people who had loved Red. They wanted to help these people they loved through this difficult time. They wanted to help themselves through this difficult time.

I fled. To the breakfast nook I went. To the breakfast nook, where I could hunt and punch, hunt and punch, where I could reread passages from the Dempsey bio, adjust the text I was producing. Aunt Filmen came to the back kitchen to see me. She was the youngest of the four children in 1914 who had emigrated from Italy. Aunt Filmen lay her hand on my shoulder.

"Come out front, Tommy," she said. "People want to see you."

I declined, couldn't look at her again after I saw her coming toward me. I told Aunt Filmen I had work to do, as I reread words on the typing paper. I had to get this writing done.

More relatives and friends came back to the breakfast nook and tried to be cheerful, were cheerful, talking to me about sports, school, and my friends. I stood them, all these people I loved. I stood them and waited patiently through their condolences so I could get back to my work involving labor and language that would keep me from thinking about that night on Route 44 near Ravenna, Ohio. It was the work, the ditch digging, I had to do—hunt and punch, hunt and punch—so I would not think.

My father and his four bowling friends—one of them my Uncle Ralph, my father's nephew—had gone to the bowling tournament that night to find that there had been a scheduling mix-up, an error on the form that had been sent out. The tournament was the following week. So there were the five men, primed for an evening out amid the din and camaraderie of a bowling tournament. But the alley was empty. It was so quiet they could hear the fluorescent lights buzzing. The men were offered a chance to bowl anyway, by themselves. Their scores would be entered into the tournament along with the other teams, but they didn't want to bowl alone, didn't want to miss the edge of competition that bowling against another team would provide.

Instead of driving back to Malvern, Daddy and his friends piled into the Cadillac and drove to Northfield Park, a premier harness racing track. They stayed for three races, then called it a night and headed home. Not far from the track, one of them shouted from the backseat, "Look out!" Headlights bore down on them.

Two men—one nineteen, one twenty-nine—were drag racing, roaring side by side down the public road, their cars somehow locking together. They plowed head-on into my father's new Cadillac. I imagined the explosion of metal must have lit up the road for a moment. One speedometer of the drag-racing cars was pegged at eighty-three miles per hour. The thought of a collision at, say, 140 miles per hour made me wince. It still makes me wince. Everyone was injured badly. Broken bones, lacerations, head trauma, internal injuries. Everyone was hospitalized, except my father. He was killed, his chest crushed, dead at the scene of the accident.

These were the details I sought to escape through my hunting and punching. I isolated myself in that breakfast nook to survive. I could think about this sports figure from forty years earlier, read and think about a time in America when my father was in his twenties. Imagination carried me away. An author's words provided escape. Fashioning my own words into sentences and paragraphs gave me solace. Hunting and punching let me hang on.

9

the visit

One Sunday afternoon several weeks after my father's funeral, Mom and I got unexpected visitors: Mr. and Mrs. Thompson, Billy, and Joey. They were dressed in Sunday clothes. I hadn't seen them since they'd left Malvern nine years earlier. I was stunned when I saw who was at the door.

Mom invited them into the living room. We all sat in the colonial-style furniture she had bought in the last year. Though Billy and Joey had been to our apartment plenty of times when we were children, this was the first time for Mr. and Mrs. Thompson. Mom hugged the boys; she'd always liked them. She offered Mr. and Mrs. Thompson a drink. They declined. Mr. Thompson had become a deacon in his church. I don't remember that he drank anyway. I got Billy and Joey Cokes.

The Thompsons wanted us to know how bad they felt. "Mr. Red was such a good man," said Mr. Thompson. "Such a good man." My father had always been "Mr. Red" to the Thompsons. My mother was Mrs. Red.

Although I'd rarely heard Mrs. Thompson say much, Mr. Thompson was gregarious. He sat on the edge of the couch, leaning forward, holding his porkpie hat, talking up a storm. There was an urgency, a rapidity to Mr. Thompson's gruff voice. The more he told a story or made a point, the more excited he became about his topic, sometimes running out of breath before he finished a sentence. He talked of that raggedy old house they had lived in, the privy with its stench that was brutal to visit in winter and nauseating to visit in summer. He told of the ornery things we kids had done.

He told of Billy, Joey, and me sitting on the back cement steps of the beerjoint one summer afternoon. We wore T-shirts and shorts that revealed our knobby, scabby knees. We had a hot dog stuck on a fork. I took a bite and passed it to Joey. Joey took a bite and passed it to Billy. When the hot dog was gone, I went inside the place and came out with another. I didn't tell my dad what was going on. He just thought I was hungry. When we finished the second hot dog, I got up to go get a third.

"You remember that, Tommy?" said Mr. Thompson.

I did.

"Mr. Red stood right there at the door! Just like this!" Mr. Thompson sprang to his feet and struck a pose, his feet apart, his hands on his hips. He laughed uproariously.

My mom had been cheerless and despondent since my father's death. She was emotionally numb. Her usual sense of humor and disarming ability to laugh at herself had disappeared. After a week, I had gone back to school, had experienced a forced and frightening reemergence into the world of people. Mom had holed up in the apartment. She rarely went out. Friends and relatives came to see her. That was the extent of her social interaction.

That afternoon, though, because of the Thompsons' visit, I got a glimpse of the mother I'd once had. Mr. Thompson's nonstop storytelling, his wheezing laughter, the exploits of Billy, Joey, and me as children, all these had my mother laughing, the first laughter I'd heard from her in weeks.

Since my father's death, I had carefully concealed my feelings. I didn't show them. I didn't talk about them. If adults viewed my even demeanor and thought I was coping remarkably well, that was fine with me. If someone belatedly expressed their condolences, I put them at ease, thanked them, and got away from them as fast as I could. I wasn't reaching out to anybody, and I didn't want anybody reaching out to me.

Mr. Thompson that afternoon was providing a healthy model of how to cope. Although I enjoyed their visit and cherish the memory of it today, I wasn't taking lessons then in how to cope and heal. I was desperately trying to manage that on my own and not doing very well. Mr. Thompson connected with people and expressed his feelings. He used words and stories to reawaken what mattered. It was years before I would do that.

10

the greatest book

When I was a high school junior, I read the greatest book ever written. Jack London's 1904 novel, *The Sea Wolf*. Three experiences converged to make me choose it: Mrs. R's requirement in English class that we read a book and report on it, my appetite for television reruns of old black-and-white, Hollywood movies, and my father's death nearly two years earlier.

The Sea Wolf was adapted into a movie in 1941, starring Edward G. Robinson, my favorite actor. He could play any part. He was a Norwegian immigrant farmer in *Our Vines Have Tender Grapes* (1945), a vicious gangster in *Key Largo* (1948), a comic gangster in *Brother Orchid* (1940), a brilliant physician in *Dr. Erhlich's Magic Bullet* (1940), and a wily insurance claims manager in *Double Indemnity* (1944).

In *The Sea Wolf* Robinson played Wolf Larsen, brutal captain of the *Ghost*, a lawless schooner whose purpose is theft of seal skins in the Pacific Ocean. Larsen is violent, cruel, duplicitous, and utterly without conscience. He rules the crew through fear, intimidation, and abrupt, routine violence. "My strength justifies me," he says. Larsen is also self-educated, well-read, and philosophical—shelves in his cabin are full of books on philosophy, science, mathematics, and literature. One of Larsen's favorite books is *Paradise Lost*. He quotes Milton's Satan with much satisfaction: "Better to reign in hell than serve in heaven." Larsen comes into conflict with George Leech, a defiant young seaman, and Humphrey Van Weyden, a well-bred gentleman and writer who is fished out of San Francisco Bay when the *Ghost* is just under way.

I figured the movie was based on a book. I asked my mother to buy me the paperback on her next trip to Canton. The author, I discovered to my surprise and delight, was Jack London. I knew him from previous, fulfilling reading experiences: the suspenseful short story "To Build a Fire," in which setting is all, and the adventure novel of a dog, *The Call of the Wild* (a book I also sought out because of a movie—the 1935 film of the same name, starring Clark Gable).

Though I loved the rapid pace of the movie version of *The Sea Wolf*, the novel made for greater depth, detail, and development of characters. London's *Ghost* is a legitimate sealing vessel, not lawless, though Wolf Larsen is even more vicious, brutal, intelligent, and physically powerful than Robinson had played the part.

The novel sharpened character conflict through extended discussions between Wolf Larsen and Humphrey Van Weyden, who, though just as well read as Larsen, had lived a life of delicacy and privilege. Their debates grabbed me more than the scenes of adventure and violence on the high seas. The debates skewered me, in fact, and made me confront that which had lurked about in my mind since my father's killing (I'd always considered the way he died—through the willful law-breaking of the drag racers—as a kind of murder).

"Life?" Larsen says to Van Weyden, "Bah! It has no value. Of cheap things it is the cheapest. Everywhere it goes begging. Nature spills it out with a lavish hand. Where there is room for one life, she sows a thousand lives, and it's life eats life till the strongest and most piggish life is left" (68).

Had my father's life been cheap and worth nothing? Was it of value only to himself and only to those who loved him? My family had been rocked, my mother cast into a spiral of grief, despair, and guilt. Much of Malvern, too, had been jolted into the sobriety of loss and the fragility of life from the death of this prominent citizen whose business was so much a part of the community. But the world certainly went on. Even the place opened the day after my father's funeral, through the heroic efforts of my brother-in-law, who worked day and night six days a week over the stretch of that summer before my mother finally went into the place to tend bar in August when my sister's second child was born. That forced society with customers she'd known for years began to pull her out of an emotional tailspin.

Above Daddy's coffin there had been a gilded crucifix: Christ in all his agony, dying on a cross. The way my father died was horrible, but not as horrible as Christ's death. Before the funeral director closed the lid of the coffin, after my uncle's brutal kisses, he removed the crucifix, the rosary, and my father's cameo ring—the inexpensive "wedding" ring my mother had given him in 1935 that he never removed from his finger.

Mom gave the crucifix to me. I hung it on the wall by my bedroom door. Each night before retiring I knelt at my bed, clasped my hands above my head (the way I'd seen a desperate Henry Jekyll do in a comic book version of *Dr. Jekyll and Mr. Hyde*). Aloud I said "The Lord's Prayer" and "The Apostles' Creed." These I said for myself, for my belief, my hope, my devoutly wished promise of an afterlife, where there would be comfort and no death. Then I rose and knelt before the crucifix and directly asked God to save my father's soul, to let him enter heaven, to admit him into one of his many mansions, as I'd heard my mother affirm there were. Then I genuflected.

11

church teaching,
church learning

Church made a thinker out of me, a Lutheran church. I am amazed
how I ended up in it. My father had been a long-lapsed Catholic.
My mother—ten years younger than he—had been a religious
gypsy. When she was three days old, her mother died, a girl of just seventeen. Mom was raised by her father's parents. She grew up knowing
her aunts and uncles as her brothers and sisters. They were very different from my Italian American relatives—different food, different
family customs, different religion, except for Aunt Violet, who married
an Irish Catholic and had seven kids.

During the religious renaissance of the 1920s, Mom's sisters took
her to church and to every tent revival meeting that came near Carrolton, Ohio. Once, they even took her to see a spiritualist, an American Indian who parted his shoulder length, shining black hair down
the middle.

He worked the crowd gathered in a large, warm room above a five-and-dime store. An hour into the service, his neck wet with sweat, his
white shirt stuck to his back, the preacher abruptly stopped his rhetoric and gesticulating. He stared over the heads of the audience to the
back of the room.

"There's a presence among us," he said.

The audience gasped.

"There's a beautiful young woman walking down the aisle."

The people turned their heads to look.

"She has black hair, red lips, and pale skin. She can't be more than
seventeen."

They saw nothing.

"She's right behind your chair," he said.

Mom was looking back over her shoulder, as curious as everyone to see the beautiful young woman. Her sister Leonora poked her in the ribs. "It's you, Mae."

Mom snapped around.

"Behind your chair," the preacher said, pointing to her.

Mom's hand went to her throat. Her eyes grew wide. "Me?" she whispered.

The preacher knitted his eyebrows. "I can't believe this," he said. "She says she's your mother, but she looks no older than you."

Mom swallowed and gripped her chair.

"Is this true? Is she your mother?"

Mom nodded.

The preacher's face relaxed. His bright eyes softened. "Her message is that she will always be near you."

Although Mom did not go to church when I was a child, she believed in the hereafter, and she believed that the supernatural was part of the hereafter. One place to be in contact with this spiritual part of life was church. My Romano relatives—forty-two of them—went to St. Francis Xavier Catholic Church. That was off limits, though, since Mom was non-Catholic and wasn't about to convert. She sent my sister and me to St. Martin Lutheran, a small, red brick church in a lovely setting at the foot of a hill amid tall pine trees.

I hated going. Sunday school, to my mind, was goody-goody. I never knew the right things to think or say. The church service with adults was ponderous, tedious, and utterly without humor. Well, not *utterly*. Reverend Holcomb was afflicted with a nervous tick that caused him to sniff prodigiously every so often. He was one of the worst public speakers I'd ever heard, so soft-spoken and monotonous that I wondered if he had a pulse.

I always felt out of place at the St. Martin Lutheran Church. Only three people in the congregation had vowels at the end of their names— my sister and I were two of them. No one's dad owned a bar, that was for sure. When I entered St. Martin, I felt like one of the unwashed.

Every chance I could, I skipped church or Sunday school. A real triumph was skipping both. This wasn't hard, since my parents slept in on Sunday morning. I was responsible for setting the alarm clock, picking out my clothes, getting my breakfast, and walking the ten minutes to church. I could easily handle this. That's what I did during the week, too. When I skipped my weekly visit to St. Martin Lutheran, I'd catch hell from Mom, but that didn't last long. I'd just make sure I went to church the following week.

During our seventh- and eighth-grade years, we Lutherans attended catechism. That meant getting up early on Saturday, my only day to sleep in free and clear. Catechism was worse than church. We spent it with the sniffling, tedious Reverend Holcomb. I tried getting out of catechism, too, and even succeeded in delaying it a couple of months. Upon entering seventh grade, every Lutheran began religious instruction with the eighth graders who had already been at it a year. We met in the church basement at nine o'clock Saturday mornings. There was no formal announcement about this. It was just expected. It was part of the culture. Since Mom didn't go to church and since no adult had explicitly told me to start attending catechism, I just didn't go. At school one day, Timmy, a schoolmate and fellow Lutheran, said to me, "Reverend Holcomb has been looking for you! Why aren't you coming to catechism?" I made Timmy swear that he hadn't told me about this.

In another week, someone from church finally called Mom. I had to start attending catechism, and thus was subjected to some of the worst teaching I would experience in my life. Ten or twelve of us junior high students sat around tables that had been pushed together. Reverend Holcomb stood at one end of them to conduct the two-hour class. Each week, to prepare, we had to read a lesson out of the little blue Lutheran catechism book. In Reverend Holcomb's mind, preparation meant memorization.

Each chapter contained Bible verses in bold print, indented from the rest of the text. Sometimes the memorization was a cinch. The verse might be "And Jesus wept." Most verses were longer, of course, and every once in a while there would be a killer quotation of half a page. I started memorizing the shorter verses late Friday night, usually before "Shock Theater" began. With a little luck, I could skate through catechism, even if I hadn't memorized all the verses.

Reverend Holcomb began class by asking the student to his immediate right to recite the first verse. If that kid didn't know it, sometimes he'd say so, or sometimes he'd stumble through so badly that

Reverend Holcomb interceded. He'd look disappointed and hurt, then call on the next student. Once the verse was recited to his satisfaction, Reverend Holcomb held forth, explaining how the meaning of the verse applied to Lutheran doctrine, why it was important, what the consequences were if it wasn't obeyed. We listened, silent. When he was done, Reverend Holcomb went on to the next verse and the next student. The girls usually had the verses memorized. With the boys it was hit or miss.

Once we were seated around the table, I'd count the number of students to my left, open the catechism book on my lap, and page through, trying to figure out which verse I might be asked to recite. When I saw that a short verse might fall to me, my heart lifted. If I hadn't memorized it yet, I might have time to before he got to me. Of course, you never knew how that was going to work out. Robin, Marcia, and Renee always had the verses memorized. Timmy never memorized them. Whenever Reverend Holcomb called upon him, Timmy frowned and stared at the table. He seemed deep in thought. When sufficient time had passed, Timmy grimaced, conceded defeat, and rapidly shook his head. He wanted everyone to think he'd memorized the verse, filed it somewhere, and just could not for the life of him retrieve it at that moment. He went to a lot of trouble not to disappoint Reverend Holcomb. I admired Timmy's gamesmanship.

Memorizing Bible verses, though, isn't what made me a thinker. Neither did the give-and-take of a discussion about religious issues, since there was no discussion. What made me a thinker was the three weeks Reverend Holcomb spent lecturing about baptism. I hadn't realized that baptism was such a big deal. I had been taking it for granted: a young couple holding their infant child before the altar, a little sprinkling of water, maybe a sharp cry from the baby, some words by Reverend Holcomb, and that was it, a welcome though brief respite from the tedious church service. During Reverend Holcomb's weekly lecture on baptism, I learned that Lutherans emphatically did not believe in immersion. Until those lessons, in fact, I didn't know what immersion was.

Reverend Holcomb laid out his argument: Small babies must be baptized. You can't very well immerse babies. Too dangerous. Too traumatic. Some people might say that babies don't need to be baptized, that children in all their blessed innocence are without sin. But, Reverend Holcomb pointed out, even babies showed anger. Toddlers threw tantrums. Such bad behavior were sins, were, in fact, small manifestations of Satan.

How about the elderly? Some people came to religious faith late in their lives when they were infirm, maybe quite sick. These people needed to experience the cleansing rite of baptism. Reverend Holcomb told us stories of elderly people in other denominations who had been immersed and later died of pneumonia. The idea, he maintained, was for these people to lead Christian lives, not to kill them because of erroneous Biblical interpretation.

And what about the weather? Reverend Holcomb asked. In Ohio, the lakes and streams were too cold for baptism by immersion nearly nine months of the year. Sometimes people needed to be baptized immediately. The elderly couldn't wait until the weather turned warm. They might die. How many of you, he asked us, had infirm grandparents or great grandparents? Could they survive the shock of immersion? The answer to these problems was clear: God intended baptism to be performed by sprinkling water on the forehead.

For the *coup de gras*, Reverend Holcomb went directly to the *Bible*: Matthew 3:5–7, to John the Baptist, preaching in the wilderness of Judea. "Then went out to him Jerusalem and all Judea and all the region about the Jordan, and they were baptized by him in the river of Jordan, confessing their sins."

Reverend Holcomb pointed out that Jerusalem, all Judea, and all the region represented many people to baptize—hundreds, maybe thousands. Even though John the Baptist stood in the river Jordan, he did not have time to baptize every penitent by physically immersing them in the river Jordan. That would also have physically exhausted him.

Wait a minute, I thought. The verse did say the people were baptized "in the river." Why did John have to go into the river if he didn't need a lot of water for the baptism? If he weren't going to immerse the sinners, I reasoned, he could have just stood on the bank and had helpers bring him bowls of water. After all, a sprinkle didn't use up much. I also remembered a striking color picture from one of our Sunday school books that showed an artist's rendering of John's baptismal achievement. In the painting John the Baptist stood in the Jordan, river water up to his thighs, looking off at a long, twisting line of people waiting to become Christians. Seemed to me like immersion was the order of the day.

And what kind of baloney was this about even babies being sinful and needing baptism so their souls would not be damned to hell, even before they had a chance to be somebody?

Yes, religion was making a thinker out of me. I was thinking that Reverend Holcomb was standing on thin ice, in great danger of immersion himself.

Years after I became a teacher, I thought of what a wasted teaching opportunity that catechism class had been. Every Saturday morning around that table there was an assemblage of young minds that most teachers would love to get a chance to teach. Boys and girls twelve to fourteen years old in various stages of physical, intellectual, and emotional development, all respectful and good-hearted and smart, even Timmy, who never memorized the verses (but who later, I learned, became a prominent member of the church—overseeing the catechism class, no doubt).

Yet in that catechism class there was no discussion, no exploration, no voicing of real questions we had about faith and God, good and evil, eternity and death. Just dogma. That's all the church was interested in—Lutheran party line, so to speak, such matters as sprinkling versus immersion, confessing sins en masse to yourself versus telling them to a priest in a confessional, why praying to anyone but Jesus (i.e., the Virgin Mary) was idolatry, why genuflection was pagan and not appropriate for Lutherans.

The one place in church where I did experience critical thinking, discussion, and debate was in the Sunday school class for teenagers after I entered the ninth grade. It was held in the choir loft. Our teacher was a crew cut young man in his mid-twenties, about my sister's age. We called him by his first name: Rick. He had known all of us since we were children. He was genial, calling us each by name, asking about events at school.

We used a booklet of weekly lessons. The lesson usually described a scenario then posed questions about how what had taken place squared with Lutheran belief. Rick's teaching style was to get us

talking, stating opinions, backing them up. Discussion. Debate. Thinking. I didn't say much in that class, intimidated as I was by the older
students, especially the sophomore I'd liked since seventh grade, the
girl who had shown up with her brother to my father's calling hours.

One Sunday a few weeks after my father's death, Rick pointed
something out: "You know, we don't get into heaven through good
works." He let that hang a bit, then added, "How good you are on earth
doesn't mean much unless you believe in Christ. You don't have faith
that Christ is the son of God, you won't enter heaven."

It was a stark, indelible moment. Rick sat on the edge of a banister
in the choir loft, his hands on his lap, one foot dangling off the floor.
His words encapsulated why I knelt in front of that gilded crucifix each
night, petitioning God to have mercy on my father and to let him into
heaven. My father had never professed faith in Christ. I didn't even
think he had believed in an afterlife. And he never went to church.

"So if you're doing good things, that doesn't count?" I asked.

"It counts," said Rick. "God is glad you're doing them. He wants
you to be kind to others. But if you don't have faith in Christ, you won't
get into heaven."

I chewed my lower lip.

Sometime that summer after my father was killed, I began spending Sunday morning cleaning the place. My brother-in-law had been
doing that job, along with tending bar full time. But that summer he
got crazy busy working day and night to keep the bar going. My mother
was in such a deep depression, so afraid of meeting anyone, that she
didn't leave the apartment much. Cleaning the place on Sunday morning fell to me. I didn't mind. I swept, mopped, and sometimes waxed
the floor. I wiped off the barstools and the seats in the booths. I emp-
tied the trash. I filled the beer and pop coolers. I could have done the
work anytime on Sunday, could have done it after church and Sunday
school, but the tradition was to do the work on Sunday morning. I saw
no reason to change that. Now I had a legitimate excuse to miss my
weekly visit to the St. Martin Lutheran Church.

Two years later when I read *The Sea Wolf*, during one of their debates on morality, Wolf Larsen asks Humphrey Van Weyden, "By the
way, do you believe in the immortal soul?" (49).

I wasn't sure. I wasn't sure at all.

12

the danger of countenance

I.

During the summer before my junior year in 1965, we got a new head football coach. Mr. Parker was wise and much experienced. He'd been head coach at two other schools before coming to ours. In fact, ours was the smallest school where he had ever coached. He took the job because he also became principal.

We hadn't been coached in the Parker style before. He was concerned about the physical health and moral development of his players just as much, it seemed, as he was about winning football games. That was new. "Let's not leave our game on the practice field," he told us. When a player was injured, he did not play or practice until he healed. A coach from my sophomore year, after I'd tackled someone and felt my shoulder fall away, had taken my hand and twirled around my arm, willing me to "shake off" what proved to be a dislocated shoulder. Mr. Parker delivered lectures to us now and then on theft, ethics, sexual responsibility, and respect toward girls. "Don't lay with a girl on Saturday night that you wouldn't marry on Monday."

A few weeks before our Homecoming game, we held a team meeting and explained the school's traditions to Mr. Parker. Students in various classes voted for a girl to be their Homecoming attendant. The senior class, however, voted two girls to Homecoming Court. The entire student body, then, elected one of them to be Homecoming Queen; the girl who came in second would be senior class attendant. Mr. Parker adjusted his baseball cap and nodded his approval. Each girl elected to Homecoming Court, we further explained, chose a football player from her class to escort her.

Mr. Parker stopped chewing his gum. He walked to the blackboard and picked up a piece of chalk. He was incredulous. "I see difficult days in your future, boys," he said. "Girls should make lots of decisions, but not this one. We're talking about *our* team. *We* decide who represents us."

And so freshman boys voted someone from their ranks to escort the freshman attendant. Sophomore players chose next, then juniors. When it came time to select escorts for the Homecoming Queen and senior attendant, Mr. Parker stepped forward. "We don't need to vote on this," he said.

My teammates and I were puzzled.

"Two escorts have already been chosen," said Mr. Parker.

I still didn't catch on.

"Ernie and Jimmy," he said, "our co-captains. That's who will escort the senior girls."

And that was that. In one brief team meeting, a long-standing tradition had been overturned. The status quo could be changed by calling it into question and deciding to do something different. Mr. Parker's action let us taste autonomy. We voted. We changed something. We left that meeting feeling the intoxication of empowerment.

In November, the football season ended. We'd had a respectable year: six wins, two ties, and one loss, coming in second to Tusky Valley, a powerhouse that had swept the league. At our final team meeting, the underclassmen voted for the following year's co-captains. I found myself elected, along with my long-time friend, Greg Alexander, the best athlete in school. Greg was handsome, polite, built like

Adonis, and an outstanding student in every subject. The next year, in addition to being co-captain of our championship football team, he would be vice president of the senior class and president of the Honor Society. Greg was also black, the only black student in our class of twenty-nine.

Next fall, our team gathered to choose escorts for the 1966 Homecoming attendants and Queen. I waited in anticipation. The class behind ours had accomplished a rarity that year. It had elected a popular African American girl as junior attendant. The junior boys on the football team chose a black player to escort her. Now it was time for the seniors. To my mind, a precedent had been set the previous year: the co-captains—Greg and I—would escort Amy and Debbie, two white girls. When it came time to select the senior escorts, however, Mr. Parker said nothing about any precedent. This year we voted. No one said anything. Not Greg Alexander. Not any of the players, including twelve black players on the team. Not me.

Greg was not elected. I was and so was a boy whose girlfriend had been voted queen. This was 1966. The junior class might elect an African American girl and boy to represent them, but race still mattered in our Ohio community, a village with a population of 1,352 protestants, Italian Americans, and a small African American community on the edge of town.

II.

On a Martin Luther King Jr. holiday some thirty-plus years after the incident, I telephoned Greg Alexander, who lived in South Carolina, where he was human relations manager in a prosperous textile firm.

"Oh, yes," said Greg, "I remember. Amy came to me after the decision and told me that it was a load of crap. She had talked to her mother and father, and they said they had no objection to me escorting her. Amy didn't have a problem with it, either. She was ready to take a stand, but I didn't want it to get out of hand."

Amy, in fact, had taken a stand. In a letter to me, she explained what happened:

> I went to Mr. Parker's office to request Greg as an escort. He proceeded to tell me NO. This was impossible. He was not allowed. I continued to argue with him until he became very upset with

me and then threatened to remove me from the homecoming court.

Greg had gone to see Mr. Parker, too. He went alone and in his respectful, forthright way, I'm sure, confronted our coach and principal. Mr. Parker apologized, Greg told me, but said that he didn't think the community was ready for an African American boy to escort a white girl. "I understood," said Greg, "and I felt better after the conversation with Mr. Parker."

I've thought often about that team meeting to select the escorts. But after talking to Greg, I thought about it in a new way. Now, a mirror is part of the memory, a mirror in which I see a reflection of myself. What I see shames me. During the entire year running up to the 1966 Homecoming game, I knew that the co-captain precedent of our junior year was going to precipitate a dilemma. I knew it even before Greg and I were elected co-captains after the season. Ten months later at that team meeting our senior year I thought, "Let's just see what happens." What happened was that nothing happened. When the precedent was tacitly bypassed, and Mr. Parker proceeded to call a vote, everyone was silent. What bothers me most is that I was silent. I was four months shy of eighteen.

Though my father had been mute on the subject of race relations, my mother taught and modeled tolerance and respect for the African Americans in our community. The first six years of my life my primary playmate was Joey Thompson. All through my schooling I had been in classes with black children and played on sports teams with the boys from little league on. I knew them, relied on them, admired them. And, still, at that meeting, I kept quiet.

It wasn't my problem, I thought. That's the way things were. To follow the precedent that Mr. Parker had set the year before would have set another precedent in the community. But it didn't happen. Just let things work out as they will, I thought. That was an easy attitude for me to take. I was privileged in that community, and especially in that school. I was popular with teachers and a leader on the football team. My skin was white. It didn't matter whether we voted or went by the precedent of the previous year. Either way, I would escort one of the girls. Greg was popular, too. Every teacher liked him. He was a leader athletically and academically. But he would not escort one of the senior girls at the

Homecoming ceremony. The reason he would not was because the girl was white and he was black. The more insidious reason, I realize now, was systemic racism, racism so deeply soaked into America's culture that it was largely invisible, unless you were the victim of it. And we were all victims of it, whether we knew it or not. The consequence for white people was not immediately dramatic as it was for black people. The consequence for white people was the compromising of their integrity, the blunting of their sense of justice, equity, and fairness.

I've never considered myself prejudiced. Now I wonder. Despite all my positive experiences in athletics with black kids as teammates, despite my good-natured accepting relationships with them, deep down, right at the core, did I believe that my white friends and family were better than the black kids on the edge of town? Deep down, did I believe that it was unthinkable for a black male to escort a white female at a school event? If Mr. Parker had boldly moved and named Greg as an escort by virtue of his status as co-captain, how would I have acted? With that same passivity? With a feeling of triumph that right had been done? Or would I have felt that Mr. Parker was wrong? And how important was it to my teenage ego that I be on Homecoming Court? That's a question I can answer: plenty. I never even considered giving up my own spot as escort. In my teenage mind, social status trumped social injustice.

III.

My mother used to tell this story: When I was about to turn five, she organized a birthday party for me. I invited the kids in the neighborhood, which included, of course, Joey, and his older brother, Billy. One mother informed her, Mom told me years later, that some of the parents would not permit their children to attend the party if Billy and Joey were invited. She said that she explained the situation to me and asked me who I wanted at the party. I wanted Billy and Joey. My mother was always proud of that. I have no memory of the birthday party. What I do have is a Polaroid photo of Joey and me, sitting one behind the other in our apartment above my dad's tavern, smiling into the camera. I don't know if it was taken at the birthday party. What I do know is this: Joey and I were buddies.

How, then, twelve years later, did I come to the point of passivity in the face of clear racial prejudice? When did I give up my sense of equality in matters of humanity? Did I lose it when the Thompsons moved from Malvern and I lost that daily contact with them? Did I lose it when I became a teenager and began to be interested in girls and no longer spent time with my black friends in high school? Did it happen because after school and after sports practice, the black kids and white kids socialized separately, a kind of segregation unlike the clear race lines drawn in the South, an unspoken "you go with your kind, I'll go with mine"?

I can't say for sure. Maybe I just needed to ferment longer in that systemic culture of racism to end up quiet in the face of what I knew was wrong. But here is what shames me most, even more than my silence at that meeting: I never said a word to Greg. I never told him that I, too, knew that race was the reason why the precedent had not been followed. And I did know. I was not ignorant or naive about what was happening. My silence made me complicit.

I told a colleague about this incident, expressed the feelings of guilt and shame I felt even these many years later. He urged me not to be too hard on myself, pointed out that times are different now. His urging came when I wondered aloud if the word *racist* applied to my behavior in 1966. No, said my colleague, *racist* was too strong. Racists seek to harm people because of their race. But I wonder . . . wasn't systemic racism what blinded me from empathizing with the hurt that Greg Alexander must have felt? Wasn't the black community in Malvern harmed by not getting a chance to be proud of Greg's popularity among his peers and teachers? Weren't black youth of the community deprived of seeing achievement in the success of Greg Alexander and realizing that his success and acceptance were possibilities for them, too? My colleague said that maybe a more accurate word than *racist* was *oblivious*—that many white people were simply oblivious to the harmful effects of racial injustice. I am, no doubt, oblivious to a great deal. In 1966, however, even at seventeen years old, I was not oblivious to what went on at that team meeting. I knew.

IV.

At Miami University where I teach now, my students, mainly white, are studying to become high school English teachers. When I told one group this story, they were rapt. I knew they heard lectures and engaged in plenty of discussions about diversity. I knew they saw films about it, read about it, and spent time working in classrooms in nearby urban schools, where the African American population is sometimes 90 percent. Some students say they are sick of hearing about diversity. They aren't prejudiced, they say. Racial injustice is not a problem they caused.

But my students listened to my story, and I taught them a word that had wormed its way into my consciousness: *countenance*. Many of the students, heavily prepared in literature, knew the definition of countenance that meant "facial expression." None of these college students, though, knew the definition of countenance that had been stinging me and stings me still: the verb form of countenance that means "to approve" or "to sanction."

My silence at that team meeting had countenanced racial discrimination. By saying nothing, I sent the message that I did not object. By saying nothing to Greg, my friend since grade school, I sent him the message that what had happened was okay with me. And the fact that I did not know until more than three decades later that there actually had been talk about what had happened at that team meeting, that Amy and Greg had each confronted Mr. Parker, tells me how others perceived me then. My silence told them that I was not an ally. They would not share their sense of racial injustice with me. They would not include me in planning a course of action. I was president of the senior class and co-captain of the football team, yet I was unaware of the courageous acts on the part of two of my peers.

Where I faltered, Amy and Greg stepped forth.

I commend their courage and moral rectitude.

V.

Because I am a teacher of future English teachers, I can't help wondering about another part of my high school education. I wonder if something could have been different in the curriculum, even in 1966, that might have prompted me to speak against what I knew in my bones was wrong. The literature curriculum of my English classes then represented a white perspective on human experience. Except, perhaps, for James Weldon Johnson's poem, "The Creation," I remember reading no fiction, nonfiction, poetry, or drama by African American writers. No Langston Hughes, no Gwendolyn Brooks, no Ralph Ellison, no

Countee Cullen, no Zora Neale Hurston, no Richard Wright, no So-
journer Truth, no Frederick Douglass. No Harlem Renaissance. There
was a body of African American literature out there. We read none of
it. I don't even know how much of it was contained in our American
literature anthology.

In 1961, *To Kill a Mockingbird* won the Pulitzer Prize for fiction. We
didn't read that in school, either. It was being read by others, though.
My girlfriend had read it in a neighboring school—an all-white school.
Although written by a white author, even *To Kill a Mockingbird* would
have given us students an opportunity to think, write, and talk about
social justice, racism, community mores, and moral responsibility. And
it is the talking that is important. During the summer before my senior year, I read *To Kill a Mockingbird* at my girlfriend's recommenda-
tion. The novel absorbed me. I felt the injustice of Tom Robinson's trial
and death. I admired the integrity and courage of Atticus Finch. But
that sympathy and admiration wasn't enough to move me to speak at
that team meeting a few months later.

I didn't talk about the book with anyone. I didn't talk to my girlfriend about it when she returned from vacation. I didn't talk to my
friends. I just liked the book, found it fulfilling—a fictional dream that
let me vividly inhabit a world three decades earlier in a southern town
in Alabama, where morality and integrity and conscience were tested
around the issue of racism. Literary critic and teacher, Mark Edmundson,
maintains that if we teachers hope that literature will be part of students' moral development, getting them simply to enjoy important
works of literature is not enough.

> Taking a deep initial delight in a book or an author is a little like
> falling in love. There is nearly rapturous acceptance of all the au-
> thor brings. The truth unfolds as if from above. But to adapt that
> vision to one's own uses, to bring it wisely into the world, more
> than love is necessary. One also has to apply a critical scrutiny to
> the work—consider its connotations, examine its antecedents,
> asking always: What would it mean to live this vision? (2004, 94)

That's what talk can do, even talk that is not necessarily led by a
skillful teacher. Students, Edmundson writes, "are in dire need of maps,
or of challenges to their existing cartography . . . they seek ways to un-

fold their promise, to achieve the highest form of being they can (2004, 136).

I attest to that. As a teenager I sought answers. I wanted to probe big questions—about death, about life, about love, about friendship and loyalty, about right and wrong, all this amid the peer pressures of popularity and ranking, the tension between tradition and change, the systemic racism so resistant to reform.

Teachers have the opportunity to get teenagers talking about literature—in small groups and in large groups. If teachers can develop classrooms of openness to opinion and exploratory thought, they will give students opportunities to hear different voices connecting the events of a particular piece of literature to their own times. The explanations of thinking, the discussion, the argument and debate, the staking out of some moral ground and testing it in the presence of peers, however painful, makes for growth and development.

It takes a skilled teacher to manage such a classroom. Maybe I'm pipe dreaming here to believe that the study of literature affords students the opportunity to become socially conscious, indeed, to become socially active. Still, had I been in a classroom where conversations about race had been sparked by the lives and moral dramas in literature, conversations and some writing in which we reflected upon our personal experience growing up in that largely white town with a small black population on the fringe, in which we connected that with some of the history of race and social justice . . . might that not have moved me, just a little? Might that not have stirred more uneasiness in me, made me resurrect the image of Joey Thompson and how much he had meant to my childhood? I want to believe that it might have, that it might have sped along my awareness, that it might have turned my apathy to action in speaking out against a clear example of racial discrimination, even at seventeen, especially at seventeen.

VI.

Thirty-one years after that team meeting I sat on a front porch talking with a good friend from those high school days. Kurt had played center on the football team and had married a bright, pretty girl in the class behind ours. Jill was voted Homecoming Queen the next year. Kurt and I sipped cold drinks and looked out over the quiet, tree-lined street he lived on, just two blocks from the high school. I asked Kurt if he remembered choosing the escorts in 1966, the ignoring of the precedent that had been set the year before. He did. I offered an opinion: "Mr. Parker just didn't have enough courage then to sanction a black football player escorting a white girl."

"He had enough courage the next year," Kurt said.

I raised my eyebrows.

Kurt explained to me how the next year, the two co-captains, Nick, white, and Leroy, black, had both escorted Kurt's girlfriend during the halftime Homecoming ceremony. Down the middle of the football field toward the bleachers Jill had walked with her right arm through Nick's and her left arm through Leroy's. She was presented with flowers. She took them with her right hand, cradled them in her arm. And there she stood, facing hundreds of community members. On her right, the flowers and the white boy. On her left, her arm through his, the black boy. In 1967, in a northeastern Ohio town, population 1,352. There were 119 students in grades 9 through 12 with less than 10 percent of them black.

As Kurt told me the rest of the story, I was revising my estimation of our coach.

"Parker made the right decision," I said, "a courageous decision."

"He did," said Kurt. "He was right, but I had a hard time with it then."

When I made that phone call to Greg Alexander, I asked him if he knew what had happened the following year with Jill, Nick, and Leroy. He didn't. I told him.

"Do you think that was Parker's doing?" I asked Greg.

"If it wasn't, he must have had a hand in it."

The decision at the team meeting that excluded Greg must have bedeviled Mr. Parker's sense of morality for an entire year. And I'm betting that Greg's and Amy's courage at seventeen years old to confront their respected principal and coach had caused Mr. Parker to face the issue further, had kept that bedevilment alive. More talk. More debate. More reflection. Given a second chance, Mr. Parker would do the right thing. He would lead. He would not countenance discrimination. He would show the community what a move for racial justice and social equality might look like in a small Ohio community in the late 1960s when it conducted one of its rituals.

2

College

13

wayward beginning

The teacher looked out at the ten of us in Freshman News Writing, a one-hour introductory course at Miami University in 1967. He held our stories from the week before. "Time . . . is not . . . important," he said. "It does not belong in the lead. How often must I say that?"

He rose from his chair and walked to the doorway. "I'm not telling you again." He turned to the metal waste can and gave it a rattling kick. It bounced against the wall and tipped over. "Understand now?"

My ears burned. I was the student who kept putting *time* in his leads. From my ducked head I looked up just enough to see the waste can rocking on its side, balls of paper spewed on the floor.

I did *not* say, "But Mr. Hurst, time is *when*. *When* is one of the five W's. You know, who, what, where, when, and why. That's what journalists must answer, isn't it?"

Instead, I kept quiet. I didn't put information about time in my leads again. I guess his teaching worked on that score.

Why had I declared a major in journalism, anyway? I'd never worked on a school newspaper. I'd read only the comics and sports in the Cleveland *Plain Dealer*. I didn't pay much attention to anything besides popular music, movies, and girls, even though Vietnam raged and I was only a student deferment away from being drafted.

Here's why I was majoring in journalism: A high school teacher had written on one of my verbose, adverbial papers, "Tom, you have a flare for journalism!" That was enough for me.

And the day of the rattling waste can was also enough for me to drop the journalism major. I still liked to write and I loved to read novels, so I switched to my major to English, though my "Composition and Literature" class wasn't going that well either.

But what to do with an English major?

That had been decided the first week of the term. I had come to Miami University and enrolled in a major in the College of Arts and Sciences, where a foreign language was required. No problem! Miami offered Italian! My father had been born in Italy! I knew many Italian curse words. I could already count to ten in Italian! I ate *pasta fagiole*, *calamari*, *baccala*! Beginning Italian was perfect.

The class met four days a week at 8:00 A.M. It was crowded with freshman, every seat occupied, maybe thirty or thirty-five of us. That first day, Professor Batelli taught us *Dové* and *Ecco*—*Where is* and *There is*.

"*Dové Louisa?*"

"*Ecco Louisa!*"

We caught on quickly and Professor Batelli got topical: "*Dové* Stokely Carmichael?" he asked, winking.

Some students laughed. I grinned, though I didn't know who Stokely Carmichael was. He hadn't appeared in the comics or sports.

"Again," said Professor Batelli, "*Dové* Stokely Carmichael?"

"*Ecco* Stokely Carmichael!" a smattering of students answered.

That afternoon I sat in my Symmes Hall dorm room reading and practicing the following day's lesson, whispering the Italian words aloud so as not to awaken one of my roommates dozing on his bed. (He turned out to be a language maven, minoring in Portuguese, quitting school altogether one term our junior year and traveling to Brazil.)

"I wasn't quite asleep," Jim told me later. "I wondered what you were doing. Strange way to study a foreign language, I thought."

"Why didn't you say something?" I said.

"Hey, I wasn't butting in. I barely knew you."

The last day of Beginning Italian that week, I sat in the first seat of the first row. Professor Batelli flopped open the textbook, began to go over the homework exercises. He looked to his left. "Mr. Romano, take the first one."

I ventured an answer.

"No, no," said Professor Batelli. He turned to the board, took up a piece of chalk, and scribbled some words. He looked over his shoulder. "See?"

I didn't.

"Try again, Mr. Romano."

I ventured another answer.

Professor Batelli wheeled around to the board, speaking rapidly in Italian. He doubly underlined the words and slammed in exclamation points. Splinters of chalk shot into the air like shrapnel. "Again," he commanded.

I ventured another answer.

He waved his hand. "No, no, no! Miss MacIntosh," he called.

With composure and confidence, the girl behind me quietly gave the answer.

"Yes, yes," said Professor Batelli. "That's more like it. You take the next one, Mr. Schneider."

That was my last day in Beginning Italian. By the following week I had transferred from the College of Arts and Sciences to the School of Education, where, shamefully enough, a foreign language was not required.

That's how I landed on the path to become a teacher. That's how my career began, thirty-seven years now teaching in both high school and college. What an inauspicious, cowardly, ignominious start. But there it is. That's my history; I have to claim it. I entered teaching because of ill-preparedness, thin skin, embarrassment, fear of failure, rash decision making, flight from what seemed out of my league, and capitulation at the first sign of difficulty. I am not proud.

Although my first two years teaching high school students and my first year teaching university students were rocky, over the years I have been rewarded and recognized for excellent teaching. In the high school where I worked for sixteen years, I was named the district's Teacher of the Year once and made the semifinals of the state competition. At the college level, I receive excellent student evaluations, have been recognized by the Student Government as an outstanding teacher. The School of Education recognized me with a prestigious teaching award, quite an accomplishment, I am told, in my academic division of five

departments. Miami University's Alumni Association named me re-
cipient of the 2007/2008 Effective Educator Award.

And yet there I was in 1967, zigzagging into teaching for all the
wrong reasons.

14

making the grade

A wesome are the students I work with now at Miami University, where I myself received teacher certification in 1971 and a Master's degree in 1975. Most of my students are more intelligent, more mature, more imaginative, and academically braver than I was. I realize now that I came to college unprepared socially and academically. My high school graduating class numbered twenty-nine. That first evening at Miami, 2,918 of us freshman packed into Withrow Court for convocation, more than twice the number of citizens in my hometown. In high school I'd taken three science classes (and never dissected a frog) and three math classes (where I was pretty much lost after Algebra I). I'd had only one year of a foreign language—Latin.

Before the first term, Miami sent me an invitation to be part of the "Class of '71 Photo Directory." I eagerly sent in my senior class photo, five dollars, and a biographical information sheet—my chance to show my future peers that I was somebody! I detailed my high school resumé: president of the senior class, lead in the junior class play, school representative to Buckeye Boys' State, student council, escort on Homecoming Court, varsity letters in two sports, and, my proudest accomplishment, co-captain of a championship football team. In "The Baby Book," as I learned the directory was called, the "Tom Romano entry" was composed of my name, photo, hometown, major, and residence hall. All my high school accomplishments had been reduced to "student government, varsity sports." Those activities, I saw, were a dime a dozen. So were clubs, honoraries, music, and dramatics. I was still a medium-sized fish, but I was no longer swimming in a tiny pond. And I was about to learn that I wasn't as smart as I thought I was.

That first term I avoided academic probation by mere tenths of a point. In December, I opened the official Miami grade transcript that had arrived in the mail and breathed deep relief when I saw the modest 2.2 GPA.

1st TRIMESTER 1967–68		ROMANO THOMAS S
Z00 011	PRIN ANIMAL BIOL	C
ENG 011	COMPOSITION & LIT	C
ENG 182	FRESHMAN NEWS WRTG	B
SPC 131	ESSEN PUBLIC SPKG	B
PSY 011	INTRODUCTORY PSYCH	B
SOC 021	GEN ANTHROPOLOGY	D

To succeed in college, I realized, I'd have to do more than read assignments. I'd have to study. I'd have to remember. I'd have to think.

The final grade I was proudest of was the "B" in Introductory Psychology. That course had fit the college stereotype: large lecture hall, tiered seating, hundreds of students, thick textbook, lectures that had nothing to do with the week's readings. A couple weeks before the final exam, the professor explained his "Baseball Theory of Grading." In his course, as in a baseball game, you could turn losing into winning in your final at bat. You might be down several runs. You might even be hitless—running with a strong F. But if you came through with a clutch hit on the final exam, you were redeemed. You could snatch salvation at the last moment like a crucified thief. Your grade on the final exam, the professor explained, was your grade in the course, provided it was higher than your accumulated weekly quiz grades. If you prepared for that final plate appearance, you might even knock one into the seats and come home with an A.

Unlike the thief on the cross, though, I had to do more than just say I'd had a change of heart. I had to take action. The King Library became my home. I learned that it wasn't just a place that held books. In the library I could find a cubicle on the third floor with a desk and comfortable chair. I found quiet and solitude with few distractions, just new friends dropping by occasionally to chat and the girl and guy nearby, who, every forty-five minutes or so, studied in tongues. I reviewed my psychology notes, reread the textbook, highlighted concepts and critical information. I even read the footnotes and glossary. On the final exam I hit a triple.

Of course, the B in Psych was balanced by the D in Anthropology. The rest of my grades pegged me as an average college student. I was co-captain no longer. I was just one of nearly three thousand eighteen-year-olds at Miami University. Many were striding forth, achieving academic success. Some were flunking out of college, usually because of poor study habits, a lack of academic discipline, or the lure of unparalleled social freedom. College was making me take a hard look at myself, my capacities, my relationship to others, the powers of my mind. I was struggling for intellectual respectability. That triple in Introductory Psychology, regardless that it relied on rote memorization, was a watershed moment.

Today at Miami University I direct the program for students who want to teach English. It's a permutation of the very program I graduated from in 1971. I wouldn't be admitted into it today. Admittance requires a rock-bottom 2.5 minimum grade-point average. My GPA was 2.3 when I would have applied. I can't blame that on irrelevant courses or unfair professors. I'd entered a new reality, both zigzagging and bearing down with everything I had, becoming, in the words of a new friend from Cleveland's Little Italy, a bookie.

15

exam

Thousands of first-year students at Miami University streamed over campus that warm spring morning in 1968, heading for large classrooms and lecture halls to sit for the two-hour written examination in English 012. I was doing better that semester, even though my grade in English was between B and C. I'd come to realize that I was going to have to give my studies everything I had to make it in college. I had to give what intellect I owned the advantage of hard work and preparation. I started assignments early, didn't procrastinate, and went to King Library each evening after supper until ten or eleven o'clock. I knew how to be the good ditch digger.

The first semester in English 011, students had to write different kinds of expository essays and pass the "Q-Test"—a qualifying objective test over grammar, usage, and punctuation. You could pass the Q-Test and still do poorly in English 011. But if you failed the Q-Test, you wouldn't pass the course, even if you wrote like a dream. English 012 concentrated on writing about literature. Didn't matter what your major was—music, science, mathematics, art, engineering, physical education—you were still required to learn to write critically about literature.

"First-year composition isn't what it used to be," lamented one emeriti English professor recently. "That course used to flunk out students who didn't belong in college."

Many of us freshmen in 1968 were utterly confounded by the meanings our professors professed about poems and stories and novels. Most of us took the professors' interpretations as gospel, even though they were only interpretations. Just as in science and math, many of us believed that literature had irrefutable final answers. Some of us were skeptical, say, of the Freudian analysis of *Alice's Adventures in Wonderland*, but we still filled our notebooks with the professor's pronouncements. Whenever the topic of English 012 came up in the dormitory, you would often hear in conjunction with it the word *bull-shit*. I was still learning to undo my adverbial, pseudo elevated, elite writing style that I thought was required in the writing of educated people—and that is, after all, what I was striving to become.

The weekend before finals week, the dormitory was abuzz with speculation about what poem we freshmen would be required to read, analyze, and write about perceptively and authoritatively.

I was assigned to Hall Auditorium, a creaky, old performance building that seated hundreds: wooden floors, wooden seats, and a balcony that sagged in places. I veered right and headed up the steps to a corner of the balcony near the stage. I plopped down in a seat, lifted the desk surface from the side, flipped it over, and waited for my peers to file in and be seated.

The hubbub of chatter pulsed down quickly as blue books were distributed along with the assignment and poem on a single sheet of paper:

> I know that He exists.
> Somewhere—in silence—
> He has hid his rare life
> From our gross eyes.
>
> 'Tis an instant's play.
> 'Tis a fond ambush—
> Just to make Bliss
> Earn her own surprise!
>
> But—should the play
> Prove piercing earnest—
> Should the glee—glaze—
> In Death's—stiff—stare—
>
> Would not the fun
> Look too expensive!
> Would not the jest—
> Have crawled too far!
>
> —*Emily Dickinson (1961 [1890], 71–72)*

My heartbeat quickened. I looked over the balcony onto the hundreds of students seated below, every other seat empty, heads bent to
the poem. Occasional coughs, the raising or lowering of a desktop, seat
shifting, spring daylight flooding through windows. I began to work
with the poem, underlining words and phrases, jotting annotations in
the margins, trying to follow Emily Dickinson's stream of thought and
meaning.

This poem was about God. Why didn't he give some sign of his existence? Why was he silent? Why didn't he make it easy to believe in
him? I wanted to believe. I needed to believe. Yes, the play was pierc-
ing earnest, I had learned. Dickinson articulated my thoughts, emotions, and anxieties. It was mid-May, full spring, almost four years
exactly from the night of that phone call, of that woman's awkward,
bumbling voice, determined to tell me that Philip Romano was dead.

I opened the blue book, pressed the first page flat along the sta-
ples, and began to write. No outline. No thesis that I remember. I simply dived into the writing, trying to keep pace with the words that lined
up in my mind to be said. No revision, beyond the occasional cross-
ing out of words and phrases not long after I set them down and reread
them.

I tell students and teachers I work with today to have faith and fear-
lessness. Faith that there are plenty of words at their disposal, that
the language in them is enough, that when the gush of words comes,
as it surely will if they lower their standards and focus, they must trust
that gush, follow that language, work fast in a high-speed chase for
meaning.

Surely, I must have started to write in that pretentious, elevated way
I thought the university wanted. The topic was so strong in me, however, that I soon slipped into my own desperate, almost angered plea
directly to God. Certainly I wanted to do well in that class. English was
my major. I was not only looking for a sign from God. I was looking
for an academic sign to show me that the area of study I loved was one
I could succeed in.

Most of my fire and boldness during the writing, though, arose from
my doubts about religion, about God, my fears about death, about a
world that could strike such blows, a world where so much loneliness
and loss dwelt. If anyone needed comfort from a sure God, I did. If any-

one needed reassurance that there was purpose, logic, and love to our living, it was me.

When I finished writing, I don't remember rereading the entire essay. I don't remember tinkering with the words, making adjustments. I must have. Such rereading, tinkering, and revising had become my habit, my power as an evolving writer. Even at nineteen, I had learned through the act of writing that when I reread my words, especially after some time away from them, I thought of more to say and better ways to say it. I had learned to take great pleasure in that "other self," as Donald Murray came to call it, that other self inside writers that monitors and considers what has been written, that suddenly sees where words need to be added, deleted, shifted, sharpened, that suddenly knows where a point or a scene needs to be expanded (Murray 1982).

I descended the steps from the balcony, turned in my blue book, walked through the old, elegant lobby of Hall Auditorium, and opened one of the front doors. Outside was sunshine and quiet. Occasional birds chirping. Occasional far-off voices. But mainly quiet. I started across campus to Symmes Hall, my dormitory on the East Quad. I passed King Library where I'd spent so many hours that year, more hours each week than I'd spent in comparable times doing my work in the place. I passed the treed green space that Miami has never built upon, except for slant walk that connected the edge of uptown Oxford to the center of campus. Spring was long past blooming. Green was the color of the day, the week, the time. I was green, yet not as green as I had been nine months earlier. I took my time during my walk to Symmes. Meandered in the morning sunshine. No speed. No hurry.

A great thing had happened. I wanted to savor the feeling. Language had moved powerfully through me. Words and ways of saying had rushed forth. I had accepted them, trusted them. Intellect, passion, emotion, and deep psychic need had merged. And that had propelled language. I knew that the writing I produced during the exam was unlike any I'd written in thirty weeks of first-year composition. The words were raw and honest and rhythmic. They rose from grief and doubt and religious crisis that resulted from my father's death and from losing a girl I'd loved and learning to live with that kind of death, too.

I didn't have the word *risk* as it applies to writing in my vocabulary then. But risk is what I had taken, even though I hadn't thought about it, any more than a wave thinks about washing ashore. I hadn't written in that pseudo, elevated tone full of adverbs and qualifiers. I'd used an evolving, struggling, desperate voice—my own.

The quietness and assuredness ended when I opened the door of my dorm room. One of my roommates paced the floor, wringing his hands. "Romano," he said, jerking to look at me, "what'd that poem mean?"

I sat down on a bed.

My roommate began pacing again. "How can they give us something so hard with so much at stake? I don't get a C in English, I'm out of Miami."

He had struggled academically more than I that year. He liked quickness, efficiency, and exactness, especially quickness. He had flown through paperbacks of pop fiction while lying on his top bunk. I once asked him if he was going to study for an upcoming biology test. He said that he already had, that he was a speed reader. He failed biology first semester. Academic probation loomed in his future.

"The English department needs a massive dose of reality," he said. "They think everybody loves literature. I don't, 'least not the kind they think I should. I'm a business major." He stopped pacing, turned to face me, his arms crossed, his eyebrows raised above the black frames of his glasses. "Come on, Romano, what'd that poem mean?"

I was wary of answering. I still felt a sacredness and tranquility from the reading, writing, and thinking, from the flow of conviction and language that had passed through me in such a rush. But I put that aside and began to speak, quietly telling him what I had written about.

He dismissed my words with a wave of his hand. "It can't be that, Romano." He began pacing again. "I talked with some guys after the exam. One of them thought it was God, too. But the rest of us agreed—it couldn't be God. That would be too obvious. I'm going to talk to Dieter. He's got a lock on that course." He left the room, the door slamming behind him.

Such was the culture of reading literature in 1968 for so many of us. One right answer. One right interpretation. One way to know. Louise Rosenblatt's work in the transactional theory of reader response had been around thirty years, but it hadn't penetrated Miami's English department, at least, as far as I could tell.

It wasn't the interpretation of the poem, however, that had moved me so much that morning in Hall Auditorium. What moved me was the language that had been summoned in me, the powerful saying I had experienced, regardless of whether what I said had been right or wrong in the eyes of the teacher.

Still, I was curious to find out how my experience matched the teacher's perceptions. A couple days later, I went to his office, his cubicle packed into a room with a dozen other cubicles. He looked harried and weary, sitting by his desk, blue books stacked all around him. He retrieved mine, flipped it open, tilted it, and began to read aloud the running narrative of his thinking he had written in the margin. "Romano breaks through dry exposition!," he said. "First-person Romano emerges! Voice strong! Writing crisp!"

My heart thumped to his words. I knew I had written well. That should have been enough. But after a year of academic struggle and the realization that my writing didn't always wow others, I needed the teacher's appreciation of my words. I needed his naming of what I had done. I remember feeling a little embarrassed, which was, of course, much better than feeling humiliated. I didn't linger to chat with the teacher. I thanked him and walked out of that office into the new growth of spring with summer ahead.

16

enter Whitman

I am indebted to Walt Whitman. During my sophomore year at Miami, his writing gave me direction when I was wandering, faith when I was faithless, hope when my thoughts became grim. In our American Literature anthology, there were generous excerpts from Whitman's long poem, "Song of Myself" ([1855] 1981). Through Whitman's confident, inclusive voice I confronted my own emotions, doubts, and fears. Whitman spoke directly of big issues I grappled with: life and death, God and the soul. His writing revealed an intellect in action, exploring, marveling, asserting, explaining. He didn't speak dogma. He didn't follow a party line:

> Do I contradict myself?
> Very well then I contradict myself,
> (I am large, I contain multitudes.) (79)

Whitman made me pay attention to small things: atoms of blood, beetles rolling balls of dung, the pismire, the hum of a valved voice, the maternal as well as the paternal, the spotted hawk, the hounded slave, and the grass—the uncut hair of graves, as he called it. And he spoke directly about the specter that haunted me:

> And as to you Death, and you bitter hug of mortality, it is
>   idle to try to alarm me

> To his work without flinching the accoucheur comes,
> I see the elder-hand pressing receiving supporting,
> I recline by the sills of the exquisite flexible doors,
> And mark the outlet, and mark the relief and escape. (77)

Whitman was at peace with death? At nineteen, I didn't see how that was possible. I was decidedly not at peace with death. I was alarmed. Whitman saw life and death separated by "flexible doors." Flexibility, I knew, was a good thing. Flexibility always found a way. If this doesn't work, try that. If thwarted one way, try another. Flexible doors meant easy movement through them. Life and Death weren't opposites, Whitman maintained. They were different rooms of the same house. Movement from one to another was an outlet, not an end. The outlet was a relief, an escape—and either way, the doors were exquisite. And the *accoucheur*—a word I looked up—was "one who assists in childbirth." So whether being born or dying, you were entering a new existence.

Whitman's idea of mortality was hard to reconcile with my father's death. His last moments had been horrific. Terror and panic must have shot through him like a lethal charge of electricity. But contrary to what I'd learned in church, maybe my father wasn't suffering the pain of hell. Perhaps his nonbelief in a heavenly father hadn't damned his soul. Perhaps death was only bad for us, the living, not him.

One of the worst aspects of so many funerals is that final image of the loved one we carry until we die. In my case, the image was my father, embalmed, suited, coffined, fraudulently clutching a rosary, frowning forever. Whitman spoke of that, too:

> And as to you Corpse I think you are good manure, but
> that does not offend me,
> I smell the white roses sweet-scented and growing,
> I reach to the leafy lips, I reach to the polish'd breasts of
> melons. (77)

I knew about gardens. My uncles kept them. I knew how important manure and compost were in order to enjoy green peppers and tomatoes in late summer. But my father's one wild and precious life making for good manure? Was Whitman serious? Shouldn't I be outraged at the notion? What about my father's soul? What about his life force? Whitman acknowledged decomposition, the rotting of what once had lived, the necessary movement between those exquisite flexible doors. He was not about transcending death. He was not about

beating death through a spiritual immortality. Whitman accepted death
as natural. He was writing about oneness, connectedness, cycles of
living.

> The smallest sprout shows there is really no death,
> And if ever there was it led forward life, and does not wait
>   at the end to arrest it,
> And ceas'd the moment life appear'd.
>
> All goes onward and outward, nothing collapses . . . . (32)

I found this heartening—the cycle of seed, germination, growth,
bloom, maturation, and harvest, that which once was making possible that which will come—living and dying inextricably bound. The
watchword is *transformation*, not transcendence—the corpse, the compost, the sprout, the polished breast of melons.

Whitman gave my spiritual needs plenty to think about. His ideas
were so much more companionable to me than the quibbling over how
baptisms were conducted or whether infants needed saving because
of innate sinfulness. The spiritual path I was following was not one of
conventional religious faith. Literature was meeting my spiritual needs.
The minds of fellow humans were highlighting what mattered in life,
were revealing emotions people experienced, were articulating ideas I
felt in my bones and other ideas I hadn't thought about. I was content
with that.

Whitman also affected me as a nascent writer. Up to that point in all
my writing, whether school reports or self-sponsored essays, I wanted
to be eloquent. I sought a reasoned, conservative style. Whitman, on
the other hand—this man writing a hundred years before I was born—
said outrageous things:

> I do not press my fingers across my mouth,
> I keep as delicate around the bowels as around the head
>   and heart,
> Copulation is no more rank to me than death is.

> I believe in the flesh and the appetites,
> Seeing, hearing, feeling, are miracles, and each part and tag
>   of me is a miracle.
>
> Divine am I inside and out, and I make holy whatever I
>   touch or am touch'd from, (47)
> The scent of these arm-pits aroma finer than prayer,
> This head more than churches, bibles, and all the creeds. (48)

Arm-pits aroma finer than prayer?

Keeping delicate around the bowels?

Divine am I inside and out?

A person's mind counting for more than churches and bibles, beliefs and principles handed down through generations?

Many of my teachers in grade school and high school would have called Whitman offensive. Reverend Holcomb would have called him blasphemous.

But I quickened to Whitman's ideas. He acknowledged and praised what others called indelicate and never talked about publicly—copulation, bowels, the senses. Whitman valued the body as well as the mind, the flesh as well as the soul. Each was indispensable for the life we lived.

I wanted to think in such ways, to have the courage and the mental and spiritual capacity to think and say things that opposed prevailing thought when prevailing thought needed opposing. I wanted to speak the rude truth and to speak it in a way that had substance and got attention. Since encountering him when I was nineteen, Whitman has been ever with me.

I look back now from a distance of four decades and see that Whitman was also laying the groundwork for my bedrock belief as a future writing teacher. Whitman sounded his barbaric yawp. He knew that what he was, was enough. Where he was—intellectually, emotionally, spiritually—was the place he could write from. He respected his perceptions. My point of view, too, was valid. So, also, were the points of view of my some-day students. "I speak the pass-word primeval," Whitman wrote, "I give the sign of democracy" (47).

A teacher teaches every student in the classroom, regardless of class, race, gender, religion, nonreligion, politics, and idiosyncratic family experience. As a writing teacher, my job was to get those students to sound their barbaric yawps, to speak their rude truths, and to move them along in their development of language learning and written knowing. This included students who had a proclivity to matters linguistic, whose voices were learned, literary, and sophisticated in the best sense—there are some in every class. And this also included students who struggled with spelling and conventions, whose dialects did not match standard, written, edited English. "Clear and sweet is my soul," wrote Whitman, "and clear and sweet is all that is not my soul" (29). I had a place, a rightful place, in which to dream and wonder and reflect. My students had their places, too.

> I do not call one greater and one smaller,
> That which fills its period and place is equal to any. (71)

It took many years to intellectually embrace that kind of linguistic egalitarianism. I'm still striving to do it better, more completely, more inclusively, to live it and to teach it. Whitman, I think, would understand my struggle.

17

Milton

"Say it simply, Worley."

"Pack your story with details, Kleefeld."

"It's only words on paper, Zucker. It's not about reality. It's about suspending disbelief."

"That's just the kind of upbeat ending I like to see, Cornelisse."

"You might never sell it, Romano, it's too gentle. But me? I like it. I don't care what the class says."

That was Milton White speaking, the teacher I had at Miami University who connected most personally with his students, yet he always called us by our last names. Coming from Milton, it sounded affectionate and respectful. Milton taught creative writing at Miami from 1958 until 1981. He had published three slim novels. Both his prose and his teaching were intelligent, witty, and compassionate.

I took four quarters of fiction writing classes with Milton. Of all my teachers in college, Milton most influenced my teaching, my writing, my life. In Milton's classes we didn't just read what published authors wrote about the big issues. We wrote about the big issues ourselves. We turned in one copy of our short stories to Milton and deposited another in his course folder on reserve at King Library. We came to class having read each other's work, ready for discussion.

Milton forever urged us to write about the subject matter we knew. He didn't go in for science fiction or fantasy. He wanted us to write realistic fiction out of the lives we lived and the characters we knew. That's what he did.

"You're a little like me, Romano. I have a small corner I write about. Write about your dad's bar. Write about those characters you know."

And I did. The first short story I published—one in *Dimensions*,
the campus creative arts magazine—was a story I turned into Milton's
class. Milton gave the piece to the editor without my knowing it. I received five dollars and two copies of the magazine. (I was in good company. There was a sonnet in that issue of *Dimensions* by Rita Dove, who
later became poet laureate of the United States.)

The next short story I published in *Dimensions* was the final one I
wrote in Milton's class—"Papa Owned a Beerjoint." The story sparked
lively debate about the boy's character. Criticism, opinions, and questions swirled around the seminar table. At one point the class discussed
the final paragraph:

> Papa counted the money and paid no attention to me, but every
> so often he pushed a fifty-cent piece over the edge of the table,
> onto the floor. Before he stopped counting Papa did that six times.

Milton thought the boy was being cynical in taking note of the
dropped half dollars. My peers disagreed. They thought the father was
dropping the coins purposely, as payment to the boy for serving drinks
and snacks to the men playing poker in the basement that evening.

Everyone looked to me to explain what I intended.

I protested to Milton. "You said authors don't have to explain."

"Come on, Romano," he said. "What did you mean?"

I conceded. I couldn't refuse a request from Milton. I admitted that
I intended the coin dropping to be purposeful, that the father was re-
warding his son with crumbs from the table (maybe I was being cynical and hadn't realized it).

"Tom, Tom, Tom," said Milton. "You went for the sentimental."

Maybe that was my flaw as a writer, always shooting for the
poignant, but too often missing and hitting instead the sentimental.
Milton, however, had gotten a little sentimental himself that spring
evening when he called me by my first name.

I'd never met anyone like Milton before, so intelligent and humane,
so alert to language, so responsive to human actions, so good at inter-
preting them. And I'd never seen anyone so passionate about what he
did. Milton clearly loved writing, knew about its subtleties, pitfalls, and
rewards, plied the craft himself, and respected those who submitted

to its discipline. His presence in the classroom was upbeat and engaging. He was friendly and funny and yet there was a privateness and reserve about him. He wore a coat and tie to every class. Milton was just about my mother's age. She had remarried and divorced since my father's death. I imagined what it would be like if Mom married Milton. I didn't understand then that Milton was gay and had been with the same partner nearly twenty years.

In 1996, after I'd been teaching at Miami one year, Milton died suddenly. He was 81. A better teacher—first grade through graduate school—I'd never had. In Milton's classes I learned about lean prose, language play, charm, wit, and compassion. I learned to listen for a "ping" that sounded when you finished a great piece of writing—"not a 'pong,'" said Milton, "a ping, a clear and perfect ping." I've been aiming for the ping in my writing ever since.

What I learned most from Milton, however, was his example of how a teacher might live a life, a teacher who loved the craft of writing and held an abiding respect for students. I learned that if you came prepared to teaching and gave everything to the classroom when you were working it, gave everything to your students when you were engaged with them, that often, after the act of teaching, there, too, you would hear a ping.

18

coming to teaching

I passed back the *Macbeth* tests and was about to begin discussing the answers. I was twenty-one years old. This was my last day of student teaching. Before me, were my Shakespeare students, twenty-five juniors and seniors who had gotten better and better at reading the Bard, which is what happens when teenagers are immersed in Elizabethan English, not dabbling in it for one play only. I had developed rapport with these kids. For the last ten weeks we'd spent an hour each day together, talking about meaning and characters, passions and qualities of life. When the bell rang, we would leave each other's lives forever. I found that poignant and sobering. That's why I was dismayed by the students' lackadaisical attitude this day. They were quiet and subdued, indifferent, it seemed, about Shakespeare, about learning, about me. Fair had turned foul.

Suddenly Eric hauled out liter bottles of soda. Tari produced paper cups, plates, and napkins. Jodi, wearing her cheerleading uniform, came forth carrying a large chocolate sheet cake. "We wanted to celebrate your last day," she said. "Thank you for teaching us." She set the cake on the desk. Written in elaborate red script on the white icing was the word

BAWDY!

I grinned. My ears turned red. Students cheered, laughing and delighting at my surprise and embarrassment. My mentor teacher stood by, smiling. What an exuberant end to student teaching! During my time with the students, we'd read *Macbeth*, *As You Like It*, and *Twelfth*

Night. Shakespeare's bawdiness had bonded us. I had learned about bawdy humor in Professor Becker's Shakespeare class at Miami University. I was delighted to pass on to students something I'd learned in college. As teenagers alert to anything sexual, their interest piqued to the nuances and implications of the ribald humor. They probably thought they were getting away with something, too, maybe thought it a little dangerous to encounter raciness in school . . . in a classroom . . . in required reading . . . in Shakespeare of all things! Most students and their parents regarded Shakespeare as stuffy, ponderous, and pretentious, this opinion arrived at whether they had actually read Shakespeare or not, so potent a soporific was the name to modern-day groundlings.

Students began calling my attention to bawdy humor before I could point it out.

"Mr. Romano, listen to this: Touchstone says to Audrey, 'Truly, and to cast away honesty upon a foul slut were to put good meat into an unclean dish.' She says, 'I am not a slut, though I thank the gods I am foul.' And get this—Touchstone says back to her, 'Well, praised be the gods for thy foulness! Sluttishness may come hereafter.' That's so bawdy!"

For all my doubts about my academic ability, for all the elitist notions of literature I'd developed in college, for all my wrong-headed reasons for entering education, all my zigzagging, I hadn't been long into student teaching before I knew I wanted to make my daily bread as a teacher. I couldn't imagine a better way to spend my time than teaching literature to teenagers and getting them to write. Reading and writing might have saved me, but student teaching awakened me.

As I stood by the desk in that bright classroom, eating bawdy chocolate cake, sipping soda, and talking to students, I was oblivious to how much more I had to learn about teaching. I just knew I had survived student teaching. Nay, as Faulkner said in his Nobel speech, I had *prevailed*. I fancied myself a liberal, progressive young teacher-to-be. I could communicate with teenagers. They liked me. I had the skills and work ethic to get on top of subject matter. I see now, though, that I was conservative and teacher centered. Here is what I liked about teaching in December of 1970:

I liked reading the literature, most of which was new to me. It was a rare poem, story, or book I read in college that appeared in the high school curriculum.

I liked preparing lessons. I liked developing questions about literature that would lead students to proper interpretations, which I, of course, knew and which I had come by through reading a teacher's guide. (It would be fourteen years before I heard of Louise Rosenblatt's transactional theory of reader response, even though she had written about it in 1938.)

I liked finishing the grading of a stack of student essays, which is different from liking to read them.

I liked recording students' scores on quizzes, tests, and papers, tallying all that up, and arriving at a grade (the latent accountant in me finding sureness in columns and numbers).

I liked turning on the lights at 7:15 each morning and preparing for the arrival of students. (No illusion here. I'm referring to the fluorescent lights of the classroom, not the metaphorical lights of learning.)

I liked toting books and student essays to school in the gray, Samsonite briefcase a family friend had bought me before I left for college to start my freshman year and which I had put away after using it the first day of classes ("You're not a professor, Romano. You look like a dork carrying that briefcase.").

I liked the power I had in the classroom.

I was pretty severe in those days, quelled my sometimes raucous sense of humor, and affected a studious demeanor. The first four years I taught, I always wore a tie, often a coat. I was all about being scholarly—me of the 2.2 GPA just three years earlier.

I was the classic example of the high school teacher who cares more about content than kids. I surely had my own personality quirks and intellectual limitations, but I was also the product of a teacher training program forty years ago that provided little teacher training. English teachers, the thinking went then, needed to become steeped in their content, which meant mainly British Literature, the older the better. Only one writing course was required beyond first-year composition. Likewise, only one linguistics course was required, it a transformational grammar course I got an A in and whose content still bumfuzzles me. There was little to nothing in the curriculum about actually teaching the processes of writing and reading, the two huge critical skills that teachers must learn to do. It's no wonder I didn't know how much I wanted to teach until I student taught.

As I moved deeper into teaching, maybe half a dozen years, I came to value other things, although I still liked tracking grades, reading literature, and opening the classroom in the morning.

I liked going beyond the literature anthology. The poems, stories, and essays in it whet my appetite for more, sending me to the collected works of writers to discover gems the anthologizers had not included but that I thought would appeal to students: Robert Frost's "A Minor Bird," for example, or James Baldwin's "Sonny's Blues," or e. e. cummings' "my sweet old etcetera," or Emily Dickenson's "To make a prairie."

I liked preparing students to read—"building their prior knowledge," a reading education colleague would put it. To set the right tone for "Like That," Carson McCuller's insightful short story of a girl on the cusp of adolescence, I explained to students—with the prepping of my wife, a registered nurse—what physically happens in the uterus that starts a female's menstrual cycle. The purely biological definition was primarily for the teenage boys. I wanted students to have a deeper understanding of what was about to physically happen to the young narrator that altered her emotions and perceptions. I wanted civility, too. I wanted to demonstrate to everyone in class that we could talk about any topic without snickering and embarrassment.

I liked letting go of teacher's guides and engaging with literature on the same terms that students did: just the words of the text and me—my intellect, my values, my experience with life, literature, and language. I grew to especially like it when students surprised me with interpretations I wished I had thought of, when their reading, in effect, made my own reading larger.

I liked reading students' writing—learning about caning chairs, immunizing lambs, coping with the first day of freshman year, what it was like as a child to be frightened by a crow, how it was when grandpa died. I liked seeing students gain belief in the value of their own stories. I liked seeing them discover what they wanted to say—often, in fact, learn what they wanted to say as they actually wrote words on paper, stringing together language in sentences, arriving at deeply felt information they could not have articulated in an outline prior to writing.

I liked talking to students about their drafts. Sometimes I asked questions that got them to say something that surprised both of us. Sometimes I helped them over a rough spot and watched them take off from there. Sometimes I told them directly to try something that I thought would improve the writing and increase their writerly repertoire, something that would let them see themselves writing well—developing a stronger lead, for example, showing a scene that had only been told, hitting the senses, eliminating adverbs.

I liked seeing students learn to take pleasure in fooling with words.

Now, as a college professor, I still like interacting with students amid their thinking, reading, writing, and teaching. I like getting to know these new adults who want to be English teachers. Sometimes I am able to match them with a mentor teacher I think they will click with, both of them growing and doing some pretty good living within the walls of a classroom . . .

. . . which is what happened to me in the fall of 1970, when the bureaucracy at Miami University's School of Education sent me to student teach with Phyllis Mastin at Edgewood High School. She had graduated from Eastern Kentucky University and had been teaching for thirteen years. She chaired the English department in a newly consolidated, rural district that had combined a town, a village, and a burg (Trenton, Seven Mile, and Jacksonburg).

Phyllis was smart, progressive, and widely read. She gobbled mysteries and knew Shakespeare's plays with the depth of a scholar and the appreciation of a language aficionado—Phyllis loved good puns, double meanings, and perfect word combinations that surprised and informed. Over the summer, she had led the way in designing a curriculum for the school's English program. Juniors and seniors chose from semester electives. One of them to my surprise and delight was Introduction to Writing. Rare was the high school in 1970 that offered an independent writing course other than creative writing or journalism. At Edgewood High School, writing didn't play second fiddle to literature, merely an adjunct to the classics. At Edgewood, in English classes, writing simmered on a front burner.

As a new student teacher I was naive, unprepared in many ways, misguided about the lives students led and what made real learning in language arts. Phyllis, though, made me a part of the class immediately, introducing me to the students as a welcome addition who would be teaching right along with her. She talked to me about literature and writing. There was no condescension. She expected me to know things and was eager to hear my thinking (though she thought I placed too much blame on Lady Macbeth). We both appreciated wit, humor, and language play, so our frequent talk was fun and lively. When Phyllis learned of my enthusiasm for writing, that I'd taken fiction writing courses at Miami from the legendary Milton White, she encouraged me to lead students into writing their own fiction.

In each course I taught there were works to be read and skills to be taught. Often I followed a trail Phyllis had traveled. Sometimes she nudged me to blaze my own way. She listened to my plans and applauded my successes. She also knew that I was learning and that sometimes I only approximated good teaching.

On one occasion, I introduced students to key vocabulary that appeared in a short story we were going to read. One word meant "touching," "powerfully penetrating and effective." It was a word I'd read but never heard spoken. It was, I realized, what I sought to achieve in my own short stories. I wrote *poignant* on the board and said, "The athlete's farewell speech was po-ig-nant."

"How's that pronounced again, Mr. Romano?"

"Po-ig-nant," I said, confidently. Phyllis grimaced, shaking her head, waving her hand in front of her face, but graciously waiting until the bell rang to tell me of my pronunciation blunder.

I received much encouragement from Phyllis, many wishes of Godspeed as I taught kids how to write essays, how to read short stories, and how to grapple with Shakespeare. (One thing that helped me with the Bard was the field trip Phyllis organized to Cincinnati's Playhouse in the Park to see its colorful, animated [and bawdy] production of *As You Like It*, the first Shakespearian play I'd ever seen performed, the first play, in fact, I'd ever seen other than ones performed by adolescents in a high school gymnasium.)

Phyllis also stepped in with pertinent advice now and then. The short story class was a mix of kids from different academic levels with various motivation. We read William Butler Yeats' "Red Hanrahan," a tale of magic and folklore. Hanrahan, the young schoolmaster, is confronted with a choice among *pleasure, power, courage,* and *knowledge.* He selects none of them and lets himself become distracted from his purpose of joining his beloved, who is in some kind of distress miles away. I asked students which quality they would choose to carry with them in this life. One young man chose *pleasure*. He looked toward a happy life, he said. If pleasure were always with him, then happiness was guaranteed. Students wanted to know what quality I would choose.

"Knowledge," I said. The choice came right out of my background in my father's bar and bowling alleys, right out of my academic struggles, my longing to be educated, intelligent, and scholarly, like some of the professors at Miami University I so admired.

I made my case for *knowledge*, explaining how much my world had expanded since leaving Malvern, Ohio, and going to college, where I learned about anthropology, science, psychology, and literature. In the pursuit of knowledge I was discovering how much there was to learn and how much I loved to write.

The young man, however, still voted for pleasure. Knowledge, he maintained, doesn't necessarily lead to pleasure. In fact, knowing a lot didn't guarantee happiness at all. He knew smart people who were miserable.

We made our cases while the rest of the class looked on. Nope, said the boy, he'd take pleasure. He'd get the knowledge he needed to fix his car, to do the job he eventually got, and to raise a family, but bottom line was that when he was an old man he wanted to look back on his life as a pleasurable one.

I argued with him feebly, academically, my condescension, no doubt, quite visible toward this young man who did not value knowledge for the sake of knowledge, who was, by his own proclamation, headed to a future that did not include college and that was fine with him.

The bell rang. I was disappointed that I couldn't sway him, that I couldn't rally the other students to my side.

Phyllis approached me, smiling. "Such discussions are gold, aren't they?"

"I guess," I said.

"What's wrong?"

"A lot of these students don't value knowledge."

"Listen," said Phyllis, "they don't have to think the way you do. His choice didn't matter nearly as much as his explanation."

I moped, heaved a sigh.

"That boy went toe to toe with you," said Phyllis. "His argument got stronger. You should be happy."

I shrugged. "Take pleasure, right?"

"See? You're getting more knowledgeable all the time."

I asked my wife recently if she remembered during those first months we were married and living in a one-room efficiency apartment at the Miami Manor how much I took to teaching that term. "You worked evenings and weekends," she said. "You loved it."

I did. Away from school I spent time reading, preparing lessons, and marking students' essays. My father had worked thirteen-hour days, six days a week in his bar and bowling alleys. On Sundays, he went downstairs to update the books. I vowed I would never work like that. But during student teaching, I started to. And it has continued.

Any other work I'd done meant going to the job, putting in my time, trying to do it well. At twelve years old, I set bowling pins. As a teenager, I did yard work and property upkeep at the summer home of a wealthy family a few miles out of town at one of those manmade lakes that created a real estate bonanza around it. After freshman year of college, I took stoneware off a conveyer belt for a summer. The next year I got a good union job in a steel mill, making nearly twice as much money, working as a helper on a five-man team, forging pieces of white-hot steel. If I thought about these jobs at all while I was away from them, it was only in mild dread of going to them.

Teaching, I found, meant doing substantive work before I even met with students. I had to read and think about literature. I had to think about making meaningful writing assignments. I had to read students' drafts and then be of help to them before they revised, sometimes writing comments on their papers, more often conferring with them. I had to think about what my students knew and what they didn't know and then figure out how to teach them. I blundered, succeeded, got cocky and stubbed my toe, found my way again. Sometimes I surprised myself with good, instinctive teaching moves. Sometimes I taught badly when I thought I'd taught well. Sometimes I stumbled into teaching well and didn't realize it. Often I recognized when I had taught poorly and revised that poor pedagogical draft. I taught day in and day out, zigzagging toward accomplishment.

19

living literature

S horts, sandals, and tank tops had broken out everywhere that 1971 spring afternoon at Miami University. I was taking a modern theater class to complete a minor that would certify me on paper to teach high school speech.

Even though the afternoon was warm and breezy, I looked forward to Dr. Witham's theater class. He had proven himself an excellent teacher—knowledgeable, interesting, approachable. I was eager to hear his explanation of Samuel Beckett's absurdist drama, *Waiting for Godot*. The play had stumped me. Like the two characters—Vladimir and Estragon—I had waited for Godot, too, but he never showed

Outside the open classroom windows students tossed Frisbees. Two boys pitched and caught a baseball. Here and there isolated students sunbathed or studied. In the distance, a professor sat under a tree, speaking to students gathered around her.

Dr. Witham walked into class a few minutes late. He wore his usual Levis and cotton shirt with the sleeves rolled up. He always appeared ready for work. He carried no books or notes this day. He stepped to the front of the classroom, scratched his black beard, hooked his thumbs in the pockets of his Levis, and began to speak:

"My dad was a minister. When I was a boy, my family drove across country to a convention of ministers in Los Angeles. Dad went straight to the convention hall for mileage reimbursement. While waiting in line, he said something to the man behind him. Before the man could reply, my father collapsed—dead of a heart attack."

There was no sound in the classroom. Our eyes were on Dr. Witham. Something rare and important was happening. I'd never heard a professor reveal such personal information. And his narrative, unanalytic tack was new, too. The raw storytelling was riveting.

"The summer after I graduated from college, I worked in the clubhouse at a golf course. I'd applied for graduate assistantships, but it was August and nothing had come through. One Saturday evening as I was closing, a customer came in. He was Gene Tunney, a former heavyweight-boxing champion in the 1920s. He ordered a cup of weak tea and a piece of burnt toast. I made the order, then waited while Mr. Tunney took his time eating and drinking. The phone rang. It was a university offering me a graduate assistantship."

Dr. Witham told one more story that afternoon involving waiting and an unpredictable, singular event. He never mentioned Godot or the two characters who waited. He didn't pinpoint the major theme of the play, didn't place it historically in the development of modern theater. He didn't speak of Beckett's life. He didn't even explain the meaning of his three stories. In ten minutes he was finished. He dismissed class, and we students filed out of the room, out of the building into sunshine and Frisbees and sunbathing.

All these years, nearly four decades now, those few minutes remain vivid in memory. The shape of that classroom. The figure of Dr. Witham, a little grave-looking that day. The warmth of that spring afternoon on a college campus. I went back to our apartment at the Miami Manor, called Dr. Witham, and told him what a terrific class he had taught.

It was a short conversation. I didn't tell him why I thought the class had been terrific. I don't know if I could have. He didn't ask. He just thanked me. Now, however, I better understand what was going on in me. Through Dr. Witham's stories, I understood intuitively existentialist philosophy that drives *Waiting for Godot*, the notion that randomness and chaos rule the universe.

My father's death that Friday night seven years earlier made sense. Oh, I understood randomness and chaos all right. A scheduling mix-up at the bowling alley? Drag racers on a public road? Their cars locked together so neither could swerve? Three horse races? Why not four? Why not two?

Even though none of my professors acknowledged it until Dr. Witham implicitly did, literature is about our lives. Not just the lives

of fictional characters. Literary movements and theories are what academia is about. But that isn't what matters. What matters is the blood
pumping through our veins and the indelible images we carry for years.
Literature is about the blessed senses and the power of language to
waken them. Literature is about strength and frailty, sacrifice and
hypocrisy, worldliness and naiveté, grand moments of grace and irre-
deemable acts evil. Literature is about coming to know the lived experience of others, how that living might connect with us, how we can
be sensitive to others' values and triumphs and losses.

Thirty years after that memorable class sparked by *Waiting for Godot*,
I was able to track down Dr. Witham through the theater department
at Miami University. I sent him a version of this story. He wrote back:

> Tom:
>
> I've been sitting here speechless. Teaching is amazing. We go in
> every day and do our jobs and don't stop to realize that we are
> throwing stones into a pond. And who knows where the ripples
> will go?
>
> Thank you for your kind words and thoughts. The beard is no
> longer black and the jeans are a bit thick through the waist but I
> still go in each day and throw some more stones!

This memory of teaching and learning and literature is a good lesson for us teachers of English language arts, regardless of the age of our
students, kindergarten through postgraduate school. Our time with
them counts. Our commitment to the stories played out in literature
matters. In our classes students have opportunity to connect dramatically with the human experience of others. Students can come to know
those others. They can come to know themselves.

Let's remember this. Amid our reading strategies and state literacy
standards, our thematic units and multicultural literature, our ad-
vanced placement classes and canonical readings . . . let's remember
that the reason for it all is life—the characters' lives, our students' lives,
our own.

3
Teaching in High School

20

moral outrage

wasn't long into my first year of teaching when the principal called me to his office.

"We've had a complaint, Tom."

Just one? The fact that my lessons were often over well before the bell rang? That some of my students didn't know how to read, and I was assigning stories like Herman Melville's "Bartleby, the Scrivener"? That my speech minor hadn't really prepared me to teach speech classes? That two boys had given speeches composed of raunchy jokes from comedy albums, and I had let them finish? That I was directing the fall play and didn't know what I was doing, having been in only one play myself, a throwaway farce my junior year of high school? Complaints? For weeks I'd been waiting for someone to knock on my classroom door, slap on the cuffs, and arrest me for impersonating a teacher.

"Complaint?" I asked.

"I got a call from a parent who reported that her son told her that you said William Faulkner was fucked up."

I was aghast and relieved. I didn't think Faulkner was fucked up. I just thought he was hard to read. I told the principal about the two boys in speech class, added that Missy Bertram, a stellar student, sensitive and devoutly religious, had become upset and left class in tears. I told him that during my planning period I'd called Mrs. Bertram and apologized, that she said she knew of the incident, that Missy had checked out of school, come home, told her what had happened, and was presently in her bedroom sobbing.

"You're lucky it was Mrs. Bertram," he said. "She's one of the sane parents." He said he was glad that I'd been proactive and had called her.

I told the principal that I'd talked to the two boys and that I would talk to them again tomorrow and make clear they were never to pull a stunt like that again.

He said that I ought to go down to the board of education office after school and tell the superintendent about the incident. Better for him to hear it from me. I agreed. He said he'd call the superintendent to let him know I was coming.

That afternoon at 3:30 I sat in a small chair before Mr. Stein, who sat in a high-backed leather chair behind a massive, uncluttered desk, whose surface was polished and unsmudged. The office was larger than the living room of our apartment and contained more furniture.

Mr. Stein was bald, immaculately dressed in a three-piece, dark blue suit, soft-spoken, businesslike, and courteous. Although I steered clear of school politics that first year, I knew that Mr. Stein was reviled among teachers. The union leadership had accused him of bullying, deception, and violation of due process. Two grievances had been filed. Mr. Stein had hired me, I believed, because he, too, was a Miami University graduate, and frankly, he had told me, he wanted another man in the mostly female English department. Part of my job was directing two plays. That provided another reason I believe I was hired: I knew nothing about directing plays. That might not appear to make sense until you know that the previous director had complained loud and long about the shabby production facilities and had finally resigned in frustration. I wasn't long into the job when I began to think that the school system wanted someone directing plays who didn't know enough to raise a stink.

Elbows on his desk, hands placed palm to palm, Mr. Stein tapped his fingertips together. His nails were manicured. "I understand there's been a problem," he said, gently.

I told him the story of the two would-be stand-up comics. He nodded. I elaborated on my conversation with Mrs. Bertram, how I'd assured her that such vulgar speeches would not happen again. He gazed into my eyes softly, never blinking. I told him I'd taken Missy into the hall and apologized to her, given her my handkerchief to wipe her tears.

Mr. Stein took a deep breath. He looked away, smiled faintly. He brought his gaze back to me and said. "Do you think, Mr. Romano, that most new teachers are like you?"

I hoped not. I was barely surviving. "You mean . . . liberal?"

"I mean downright disgusting!" said Mr. Stein, a sudden volcanic blue mountain.

I didn't get fired that day. I didn't get fired that year. In fact, in April I learned that my contract was renewed. But I left the school system anyway.

There is much I regret from that first year of teaching. For years I thought of writing a letter of apology to the students. In fact, a couple years later I did apologize to one of them. At Miami's King Library one evening when I was living in Oxford and teaching at a school fifteen miles away, I ran into a student from that first school where I had taught. She hadn't been in any of my classes, but she had been in one of the plays I directed. She had come to college at Miami.

"Hello, Jan," I said. I felt like I was talking to someone who had something on me.

"Mr. Romano!" Jan cried.

We chatted for a bit about how she liked Miami and how I happened to be at the library. I finally told her what a much better teacher I had become, how I really hadn't known what I was doing as a play director.

"Oh, I have good memories of your teaching, Mr. Romano."

I looked skeptical. "What on earth could I have done to make you remember me as a good teacher?"

"You introduced me to Kurt Vonnegut."

That was true. For the second play I directed that miserable year, I chose an adaptation of Kurt Vonnegut's first collection of short stories, *Welcome to the Monkey House*. I had read it over Christmas break that first year of teaching. It ranked up there among the most pleasurable reading experiences I'd ever had. I couldn't wait to finish the delightful story I was reading so I could move on the next one. When I saw the book had been adapted into a play, it seemed a natural.

It was good to know I'd had some positive influence on one student. I knew the larger truth though. I'd been less than mediocre as a teacher. Not inspiring. Not visionary. Not a teacher to all of my students.

There had been no curriculum for my eleventh-grade English classes, just a thick literature anthology. So I led students on a march through Georgia, reading literature chronologically from the Pilgrims to as far into the twentieth century as I could get, with occasional stops every few weeks to write an essay, not nearly enough writing. I assigned readings and prepared questions to lead students into what I called discussions that were really lectures with my points taken from the literature anthology's teacher's guide.

I had definite issues with social class, too. I was cordial to all students outwardly, but disdainful inside of students who didn't seem to value education or were unmotivated. And I didn't recognize students who might have become motivated had I exhibited the slightest concern for them.

I *thought* I was a good teacher, though. I thought I ranked right up there with Sydney Poitier in *To Sir with Love*. Near the end of the year I asked students to complete evaluations of my teaching. I was not required to do this by the principal. I just wanted love letters from students for my ego. I was sure, though, to tell students to omit their names so the evaluations would be anonymous.

One student began his evaluation this way: "OK, you son of a bitch, you asked for it." Then he fingered me. He said there were a lot of students I didn't care about. If you were already successful, he said, or loved speech, Romano cared about you. But if you needed help, Romano left you hanging.

His perceptions were right on the money. I should also add that the school system had left me hanging. Next to my classroom connected by a door and a wall of windows was a large, often unruly, study hall. Across the hall was the head football coach, a blood and guts tough guy in a crew cut, who was also, of all things, the art teacher. In fairness to him, though, he and the librarian were the two teachers helpful to me that year. My classroom was three long corridors removed from the other English teachers. Their lunch period and mine did not coincide. There was no organized support for new teachers. No invitations to social events. No mentor assigned to me. On one occasion the principal observed one of my speech classes. My lecture ran short. No surprise there. It was early in the morning, so the students were behaved. The principal wandered over to the windows and looked out at the football field for a long time with his hands on his hips. My God, I thought. Here comes the hammer. A strong wind buffeted the light poles.

"That's unsafe!" he said, alarmed.

He could have been talking about my teaching.

Here is the one thing I am proudest of from that year: During my planning period one morning I left my classroom and entered the hallway just as two boys turned a corner going in opposite directions. They collided. One boy's books went sliding across the floor. The corridor was empty. Both boys were my students. One, Lance, was tall and blond, a high jumper on the track team. The other, Mike, was thin, unathletic and intellectual with curly brown hair that fell to his shoulders. He smelled perpetually of patchouli oil. Mike's books were the ones on the floor.

They stood a few feet apart, arms at their sides, fists clenched. Lance was a good head taller than Mike. Mike insisted that Lance pick up the books. Lance refused, saying the collision was an accident, not his fault. Neither made a move; neither gave ground. I approached them. They might have stood there the entire period. I liked both boys. Lance had made progress in his writing recently, taking a risk, and writing an essay in his own true voice about the thrill of go-cart racing. Mike engaged confidently in classroom conversation and asked good questions.

"For God's sake!" I said. I moved between them, knelt on the floor, and picked up Mike's books. When I stood up, both boys' eyes were locked on each other. "Here," I said, handing Mike his books. He took them, never taking his eyes off Lance. "Go on to class. You're late already." The boys hesitated, wondered, I suppose, if my intervention was enough to keep them from losing face, then turned and walked away without a word.

I didn't make any peace between them, didn't do anything to increase future harmony between the "jocks" and the "heads," as the groups were called in school. I've thought since that perhaps I should have directed them into my empty classroom and at least had an airing out. But still, what I did was to show them a man not afraid to humble himself to defuse a volatile situation. I had acted unlike one male teacher I'd heard once say that the best thing to do in such a situation was to let the boys go at each other awhile to get the aggression out of their system. Let the fight go until blood appeared, then stop it. I don't know if the boys remembered that incident in the hallway, but I do. It's one bright moment from my first year of teaching.

Before I resigned, I thought there was an opportunity to stay on at the school. One of the English teachers was retiring. Why would I want to stay? I usually resist change. I'm right there with Holden Caulfield on that topic. I understood perfectly why he liked to visit the museum and see the Egyptian mummies that hadn't changed in quite some time. I asked the principal if I could give up my position as speech teacher/play director and move entirely to teaching English.

"I want you exactly where you are," he said.

Just as I'd thought. My directorial incompetence had saved my job.

There was an opening at Edgewood, the school where I'd student taught. I applied. Phyllis Mastin, my mentor for student teaching and now Phyllis Neumann, was my strong advocate. I got the job.

21

over the hump

Remember the Frankenstein monster? Those black-and-white Universal movies, ol' Boris Karloff in platform shoes lurching about the countryside, he stitched together in Dr. Frankenstein's laboratory with an arm from this corpse, a fresh heart from a recently murdered girl, an abnormal brain from the school of medicine, a kneecap from Count Dracula? That described the next job I eagerly ran to. As with Henry Frankenstein, the monster almost did me in.

A number of factors came together to create this monstrous teaching position: Edgewood, just in its third year, was overcrowded. I replaced an excellent teacher who had resigned to relocate to Texas with her family (Carolyn later rejoined our staff and became a close friend). The previous year when scheduling was done, another teacher had refused to teach lower-level students and gotten her way. Two teachers near retirement each had one lesson plan, teaching nothing but freshman English all day. If I had imagined the implications of the teaching load, I might have fled to the laboratory (i.e., graduate school). Here was my schedule:

1st Period: Introduction to Composition (juniors and seniors)
2nd Period: College prep sophomore English
3rd Period: General sophomore English
4a Period: Basic Skills (an ignominiously named course—
              "juniors and seniors who don't know an introductory adverbial clause from a predicate nominative,"
              I was told, "but at least in Basic Skills they'll be
              exposed to it.")

4b Period: Basic Skills
5A Period: Lunch
5B Period: Introduction to the Short Story
6th Period: Planning

Whoa! How many lesson plans?

Five.

How many students? No more than 150, right?

Higher.

175?

Higher.

Two hundred? That number would be absurd. Five lesson plans and two hundred students would be unconscionable.

Higher.

Why don't you tell me?

206 students.

That was just one semester. Even so, there were plusses to this irresponsible schedule. I wasn't directing plays, which lessened my feeling of fraudulence. The classes I taught I was prepared to teach, though I was learning a lot about grammar and usage and still coming to understand that I needed to learn how to help kids read. I liked the students. Colleagues were friendly. I interacted with members of the English department every day, my classroom in the middle of the English hallway. The school was air conditioned.

Otherwise, I worked like a ditch digger, a driven, supercharged ditch digger. My day: I drove twenty-five minutes to Edgewood High School from Oxford and began my first class at 7:40 A.M. From there I ran a relentless pedagogical gauntlet until my planning period at 1:35. I was so mentally exhausted from the hundreds of encounters and the keeping track all day that I rarely got more done during my planning period than organizing work I needed to take home.

I left the building at 3:00, when the official school day ended for teachers. I got to our apartment in Oxford by 3:30 and handed Kathy the car keys. She was a registered nurse at the local hospital. She worked from 4:00 until midnight. Our daughter, Mariana, a toddler then, was ready for a nap, and, thank goodness, she was a sleeper.

Once home from school, I set my briefcase on the dining room table that Kathy's mom had given us. I took what I needed from it to the simple, serviceable schoolteacher's desk, another gift, this one from friends. I set to work grading papers, making plans, reading literature, creating quizzes and tests. Sometimes my eyes grew heavy in my sedentary work. When that happened, the most efficient thing I could do was to nap on the couch. Mariana awoke between five and five-thirty. I cooked supper. Meager fare in those days—Dinty Moore Beef Stew, hot dogs, hamburgers, leftovers, but every once in awhile a terrific supper of rigatoni with our homemade spaghetti sauce (to this day, we make a gallon of sauce at a time and freeze most of it in plastic containers).

After supper, I might take Mariana for a walk or a bike ride or try to get more work done while she played by herself or with neighbor children in the courtyard of the apartment complex. I bathed her, gave her a snack, and had her in bed about 9:00.

Most evenings I went to my desk and worked until Kathy arrived home at 12:15. We went to bed. I arose again in five or six hours and began a new day. Weekends were a blessing. I slept in. I didn't shave. The bulk of the day on both Saturday and Sunday was consumed with catching up and working ahead, planning lessons at least through Tuesday or Wednesday.

When Thanksgiving break arrived, we stayed in Oxford instead of driving to northeastern Ohio to spend the holiday with our mothers and visit relatives. I worked on school stuff, getting all caught up and planning ahead. I made it to Christmas vacation. I reached my breaking point when I received word that my father's brother, Giuseppe, the oldest of the four children who had emigrated from Italy fifty-eight years earlier, had died suddenly of a heart attack. Of my Romano relatives, he had been the strongest connection to my father. I hadn't seen him since the summer. Had we gone home for Thanksgiving, I would have visited him. I had to make a change. Something had to give.

When school resumed in January, I went to see the principal.

"I can't do this anymore," I told him. "My schedule is burying me."

"Oh? I thought you were doing fine, Mr. Romano. I know the students like you."

I told him about Thanksgiving vacation and my uncle's death in December. He winced.

We went over my schedule, discussed places where another staff member could pick up one of my yearlong, half-hour classes. He'd do some checking, he said, and would get back to me.

He sought out one of the freshman English teachers, a woman nearing retirement whom I knew as a fearsome grammarian. One day in the lounge, Mrs. Market wanted to know why I taught Ernest Hemingway.

"Did you know he was an atheist, Mr. Romano? Why can't you teach uplifting authors? Why do college English departments insist on teaching negative literature? You should be teaching more grammar anyway."

Traditional school grammar was Mrs. Market's domain: subjunctive mood, nominative case, correct usage of *shall* and *will*, *who* and *whom*, *can* and *may*. She didn't teach writing ("How can students write, Mr. Romano, when they don't know the rules? They'll write fluff and nonsense. The spelling and grammar will be abominable, just abominable. I refuse to read it.").

The principal called me into his office and told me that Mrs. Market had agreed to teach one of my basic skills classes when the semester changed in two weeks.

"That won't help much," I told him.

The principal looked puzzled. "That's one less class. It will lesson your load substantially."

"I'll still have five lesson plans," I said. "I'll still have 180 students. If Mrs. Market took the short story class, now that would really help."

"But isn't short story your favorite?"

"It is. That's how desperate I am. One less Basic Skills class still leaves me with five lesson plans. If Mrs. Market takes the short story class, I'll lose thirty-five students *and* be down to four lesson plans."

It took some doing. Mrs. Market would rather teach grammar. Basic Skills was right up her alley. But she was also proud of her experience and accomplishment as an English teacher. And she was a good company player.

The first day of the second semester the principal came to my short story class, announced the change in teachers, and escorted thirty-five

students on a forced march down to Mrs. Market's classroom. As they
headed to the door, a few students glanced back at me, alarmed, then
proceeded to the lair of the grammarian.

A half-hour later, just moments after the bell rang, three students
charged into my classroom. They could have been carrying torches and
pitchforks like villagers after the monster.

"Why did you do this?!"

"How could you?!"

"Take us back!"

I explained the situation, assured them they would be fine, that Mrs.
Market was much experienced, had been teaching forty years. They
knew too well about Mrs. Market's experience. They had been taught
by her three years earlier, had become acquainted with her apothe-
cary theory of learning ("Teenagers' English is sick, Mr. Romano. I have
a big bottle of pills, a special pill for each error that ails their English.
And I know how to administer the dosage.").

The three students stood in front of my desk. "You'll be fine," I told
them. "You'll be reading and talking about some good short stories."

"Mrs. Market didn't say anything about talking."

"Everything is silent seat work."

"She's giving us weekly vocabulary words and testing us on Friday."

"We have to research every author and turn in a biographical report of five hundred words every Thursday."

"You'll be all right," I said.

And they were. They didn't talk in class, but they learned about
some authors, wrote at least five hundreds words each week, and
learned new vocabulary.

And I survived the year.

22

thriving

Edgewood turned out to be a healthy nesting ground for a young teacher in the 1970s. I grew and thrived professionally and personally. I attribute this to two things: the atmosphere of possibility and camaraderie at the high school and a master's degree program at Miami University.

The intellectual climate and esprit de corp at Edgewood was invigorating. My six colleagues in English were a large part of that. We read novels and poetry and introduced each other to new writers. We read *English Journal* each month and talked the talk of passionate English teachers. We continually shaped the curriculum. Our lead didn't come from a curriculum director, an administrator, or the state department of education. It came from us, from our own lights. We were hungry teachers seeking to learn more about our subject matter. We were committed to finding relevant reading and writing assignments for our students, and we strove to teach them better.

We talked plenty about pedagogy, problems, and strategies. This was a one-eighty from my first year of teaching. Learning was an adventure for teachers. We wanted learning to be an adventure for students. There was structure; there was autonomy within the structure. Pedagogical dreams could become reality. Classrooms were crucibles where teachers experimented. When we came to new ideas or strategies or literature, we tried them out. Teachers followed their literate passions. In classrooms they enacted their evolving understanding and philosophy of teaching and learning.

My second year at Edgewood, with just three lesson plans and a reasonable student–teacher ratio in each class, I began a slow ascent to a fulfilling career in education. Our stellar guidance counselor, Lucy

King, had proposed that I offer a semester course in creative writing. I jumped at that. That next year I taught a section of it each semester, even though I was wary of teaching kids to write poetry, since I had written little of it.

Such great writing of all kinds began coming in from the students that I founded a creative writing magazine. I remembered vividly how much being published in Miami University's creative arts magazine had done for my perception of myself as a writer. I chose a staff from students I knew who were passionate about writing. We solicited poems and stories from teenagers throughout school. I contributed writing that my students did, just as Milton White had done for me in passing on my stories to the editor of *Dimensions*. The staff chose a name for the magazine—*Menagerie*—which meant a collection of wild animals, or a diverse, exotic, or peculiar collection of people. That was *Menagerie*, all right.

We published our first volume in the spring of 1974. Girls from the secretarial class typed the writing on stencils and copied them. An art student designed a colorful, appealing cover, which was silk-screened for each issue. One afternoon three students and I drove to the county board of education office, where we spent several hours hand making each issue, collating the pages and using a nifty, manually operated machine that punched holes in the pages and bound them with a plastic spiral.

The first piece of the first issue of *Menagerie* was a haiku:

> Little see, have tall trees
> Kept you hidden from the sun
> So you could not grow?

I spotted the typo the first time I opened the magazine. Most readers thought that the author was being poetic, the "little see" being a metaphor for little observations that might someday transform into big visions. Thank goodness for reader response.

The second thing that made this time as a young teacher such a stimulating one of growth and accomplishment was graduate school—full time for three summers and a course at night each semester during the school year. Phyllis had finished her Master's degree at Miami before I returned to Edgewood. She spoke highly of the English Department's MAT program, particularly courses she took from Wayne Falke. I was resistant. The last thing I wanted to do was to go back to college. My undergraduate education had been productive but onerous. Much of the literature I had read had little to do with my job as a teacher of high school students. Now, I wanted to read and write what I chose to read and write. I wanted to pursue learning that would help me teach better. I didn't need more formal education to do that.

The summer of 1973, however, I was back in classrooms at Miami. I shied away from a degree in the English Department. As much as I loved John Keats, Walt Whitman, and William Shakespeare, as much as I respected Herman Melville, John Milton, and William Blake, I didn't want to spend my time reading their ilk and being taught by professors who had never worked with teenagers that resisted reading at every turn.

I wanted to read modern American literature. I wanted to write. Miami's Department of Teacher Education offered a master's degree for certified teachers that was flexible with a modicum of requirements, the emphasis being on teachers tailoring their programs to meet their needs. Six courses were required in the school of education, four of them mandatory. The remaining hours of the degree were to be taken in English. No particular courses required. I could take whatever I wanted. What a feast! I took two classes in modern American literature, a Hemingway seminar, two classes in teaching language and literature in public schools, and a creative writing workshop that enabled me to work with Milton White again.

Two years of teaching had revealed to me skills and knowledge I needed in order to become a better teacher: I learned about language usage and dialects in America, which broadened my notions of so-called proper English. I learned about poetry by African American writers. I continued to write papers that included substance and my own authentic voice (determined was I to maintain my voice in the midst of academia). I learned about Hemingway's strengths and limitations, his vision and blindspots, his dedication to the craft of writing. I learned more about teaching reading, particularly how I might motivate teenagers who were loath to open a book ("Aw, Mr. Romano, I don't want nobody to see me carrying a book. I'll look stupid."). In one independent project I gathered strategies for teaching teenagers to write poetry—I began to write poems myself. I took electives in the Department of Educational Media: Film Communication in which I learned how film makers communicated through camera angles and distances, lighting, color, images, and editing (the life blood of film, I came to call it). I took a filmmaking course in which I planned, shot, and edited my own Super-8 productions.

A colleague now at Miami tells me that the days of such flexible master's degree programs in education are over. It's a shame. Choice works magic for teachers just as it does for students. My master's degree coursework directly influenced the curriculum I taught, my methods of teaching, and thousands of teenagers in southwestern Ohio. Miami can be justly proud of that.

I read *Hooked on Books* (1968) by Daniel Fader and Elton McNeil. The authors reported on a program for reading and writing established at a penal institution—W. J. Maxey Boys' Training School at Whitmore Lake, Michigan (19). The program got the boys to write by having them keep journals and got them to read by surrounding them with inexpensive paperback books. *Hooked on Books* transformed my Basic Skills classes at Edgewood.

I instituted journal keeping that fall to promote writing fluency in students. I wanted students to develop the habit of putting words on paper as naturally as breathing. I didn't grade journals for correctness. I graded for volume. Language abundance was what I sought. The idea sounded so good that I bought one of those hard-backed college composition books and began keeping a journal myself. I became a devotee of journal writing. I wrote religiously, capturing my feelings and thoughts, articulating my core beliefs, rendering indelible moments from my life. And finally, after nine years, for the first time, I wrote about the death of my father.

Hooked on Books, plus the graduate course I took in secondary school reading, led me to revise the independent reading component of Basic Skills. Just as I was convinced that we improve our writing through doing plenty of it, I was also convinced that we improve our reading through gaining a lot of practice at it. I collected a dollar from each student, chipped in money of my own, and bought as many paperbacks of young adult (YA) interest as I could. Students also ordered from book clubs, where they made their own choices. The more books students ordered, the more bonus points I earned to buy additional books. Soon I had a large classroom library of paperbacks.

I proposed a film communication course for our curriculum, patterned after the course I'd taken at Miami. We offered three sections of it the fall of 1975. I bought my own Super-8 movie camera and editing equipment. I made films that I used in my teaching. I made documentary films of the football, basketball, volleyball, and cross-country teams—the athletic department, I found, was generous with financing. I made a film of Edgewood Thespian Troupe 591 as it mounted a production of "A Midsummer Night's Dream." I had large built-in audiences of students, their families, and teachers when I showed the films at banquets and celebrations.

The curriculum director and I secured a grant from the Ohio Department of Education to fund a filmmaking course. I bought cameras, viewers, and splicers. The following year students learned to storyboard, shoot, edit, and add musical soundtracks to their own films. Each spring in the cafeteria we held a student film festival: an evening of teenage ingenuity, imagination, occasional orneriness, pop, rock, and country music, and, of course, freshly made popcorn and soft drinks. The money we made went toward buying equipment.

In one graduate course at Miami I wrote a driving argument out of my research and personal experience, articulating and consolidating my beliefs for teaching literature. I always tried to write with my sights beyond the course. I sought to reach an audience of those who might be interested in what I was interested in. I got an A on the paper. There was one minor correction: I'd written "in the same token." The professor pointed out that the phrase was "by the same token." At the top of the first page he wrote a few words noting that my essay was rich in examples. Not much encouragement, really, but I had faith that what I'd written was important for others to read. I mailed the article to *English Journal*. Editor Steven Tchudi rejected it, but sent me an encouraging letter and enclosed a list of the publications of NCTE affiliates.

I sent the article to the *Ohio English Bulletin* with this bold cover letter to the editor:

My dumb brother-in-law once asked me why I taught literature. He claimed it was useless. I answered him with unconvincing platitudes. I was fresh out of college then.

Since that time I've been formulating my reasons for teaching literature. Last summer in a graduate course I got the chance to put my reasons for teaching literature into an essay. Now I'm armed and ready for my brother-in-law. Please consider "Artifact and the Language Arts Teacher" for publication in *Ohio English Bulletin*.

The editor wrote back:

Thank you for submitting your article. We will be happy to use it in a future issue, probably March.

We will send you three copies of the issue. Maybe you can give one to your dumb brother-in-law.

That was my first professional publication, spring 1975. The hard, intellectually and emotionally satisfying work of the writing had paid off. The risk I'd taken in the letter, revealing my sense of humor and the dilemma many English teachers feel, had worked, too.

The lessons: Choice matters. Pursue your passions. Gnaw that bone. Keep faith. Failure is instructive and often leads forward to success. Accomplishment is often collaborative. The support of others is crucial. And as I learned from my fulfilling master's degree experience, sometimes we are dead wrong about what might be best for us.

23

zeal

'd learned a great deal from that first year of teaching and directing plays. I'd learned that the classroom is a social situation different from the beerjoint and the bowling alley and the dorm, where a certain degree of civility in speech and subject matter was necessary to getting on with the business of teaching and learning among students with different manners, sensibilities, and religious faiths. I'd learned that uttering certain words in the classroom could be explosive, the repercussions traveling through the student body and out into the community, often becoming unrecognizably transformed (e.g., William Faulkner was fucked up—if indeed my principal had been leveling with me and not offering me something so outrageous that I'd gladly reveal some other transgression).

The problem I had defining appropriateness in reading and writing for high school students came out of my own reading and writing. One of my personal goals was to read as many modern American novels as I could. I loved Kurt Vonnegut and Joseph Heller, John Steinbeck and Ernest Hemingway. I admired James Dickey's *Deliverance*, Richard Wright's *Black Boy*, Ken Kesey's *One Flew Over the Cuckoo's Nest*, and a new fiction writer—Harry Crews. I embraced new journalists like Tom Wolfe, Hunter Thompson, and Truman Capote. The characters those authors depicted often used slang and profanity. The authors wrote of topics that school shied away from: sex, war, racism, murder, drugs, social inequity.

I sought to write fiction and kept a journal in which I wrote about the life I had lived in my father's bar and bowling alleys, the characters I'd met there, the experiences I'd had in high school. I tried to write the truth honestly and vividly. My limited, little world of experience was valid. I wanted to follow Whitman's dictum to sound my barbaric yawp, not to press my finger to my lips and keep silent about all that I knew of humanity. I wanted to keep learning about people, all people, not just those living proper lives with proper speech and proper experiences. That's what the writers I admired did.

I asked my students to write honestly, too. They did a lot of narrative writing in those days, case studies and childhood remembrances, as Ken Macrorie described in *Writing to Be Read* (1975). I wanted students to write about what they knew just as the authors we read had done. I wanted my students to respect their subject matter, as Milton White had wanted us college students to do.

"Mr. Romano," said one of my students, "does that mean we can write swears?"

"Well," I began—talk about tricky territory—"in capturing a character's speech, you might find you need to use slang or profanity. Be judicious in your own narrative voice, though, and keep it clean." And yet I knew that literature was rife with profane narrative voices.

When I began to teach at Edgewood High School, I ran into the librarian, Ms. Comstock. In the library there were a lot of no's: no loitering, no talking, no gum chewing, no checking out of controversial books unless you were eighteen or had a signed note from your parents. And just in case you intended to read any questionable book while in the library, Ms. Comstock kept such books in her glassed-in office on a separate bookshelf almost out of reach. Who decided if the book was questionable? She did. On the shelf were *The Grapes of Wrath*, *The Catcher in the Rye*, *For Whom the Bell Tolls*, *The Bell Jar*, and many more.

In spring of his senior year, in my Basic Skills class, Randy was miffed because Ms. Comstock would not permit him to check out *The Catcher in the Rye*. "I'll be 18 in a couple weeks," said Randy. It was one in the afternoon, and his five-o'clock shadow had already appeared.

My classroom copies of *Catcher* were checked out. I offered him Salinger's *Franny and Zooey*.

He declined.

A couple weeks later, Randy sat in his usual seat by the classroom door, reading *The Catcher in the Rye*. He didn't look happy.

I stopped by his desk. "You got the book."

"Kinda."

"Kinda?"

"Look." He handed it to me. I leafed through. On each page, words and phrases were blackened with a permanent marker. Almost every page had at least one defacing—a *bastard* here, a *goddam* there, a *Chrissake* every once in a while. In the part where Holden recounts his meeting with Sonny, the young prostitute, the page was blackened plenty.

"And you know what?" said Randy. "All that marking doesn't do any good anyway." He took the book from me, separated a page, and held it up to the light. I'll be one phony bastard if the filthy words weren't plainly visible!

"I'm eighteen," said Randy. "I can vote. She still made me bring a note from home. And then I get this!"

Ms. Comstock had spent a lot of time going through every page of the novel, blacking out every word, every scene she deemed offensive, improprietous, licentious. I wondered if she had enjoyed this last reading of Holden's quest to protect others from the bad things in life. What irony! Ms. Comstock and Holden had common purpose.

Her censorial zeal, I learned, had even greater reaches. Ms. Comstock sent me a note, announcing that the library had purchased a number of books about film. She thought I'd be interested. I was.

One book was a beautiful little thing, oblong in shape to accommodate the dozens of movie stills it used. The text was visually appealing and full of pertinent information about the development of film as an artistic medium. There were little surprises now and then. The authors had used the margin on the right side pages, for example, to demonstrate how the eye perceived motion out of a series of still pictures. A human figure—two inches high—appeared there. On the page behind it, the human figure appeared again in the exact location but in a slightly different position. This progression continued for thirty pages. When you flipped them, the human figure moved fluidly. It was a simple and dramatic demonstration of "persistence of vision," that basic principal of the human eye that enables film to work.

The book presented a problem for Ms. Comstock, though. For the human figure, the authors had gone into the history of film and used an image from the nineteenth century, one of photographer Eadweard

Muybridge's studies of motion: a series of photographs of a nude woman descending a stair and turning around. Ms. Comstock was intrepid. She fixed the nudity with her trusty marker. On every page she gave the unclad woman a matching black bra and miniskirt. Muybridge had reached for art. Ms. Comstock achieved risqué pop. The ensemble was actually quite sexy.

Ms. Comstock was good at passing on catalogs to faculty and urging us to order materials and media we could use in our classes. She sent me a catalog from Caedmon, a company that specialized in recordings of authors' voices. There I ran across an LP titled "Hemingway Reading." I was so excited. I had been a Hemingway devotee ever since a college professor had sent us to the stacks of the old Alumni Library to read two Hemingway short stories that had knocked me on the seat of my pants. In my American Literature class I taught "Soldier's Home," "The Battler," and "Big Two-Hearted River." We saw a superb documentary on Hemingway, narrated by Chet Huntley. During my master's degree work, I had taken a Hemingway seminar and read just about everything he had published, save his journalism. Yet I had never heard his speaking voice. I told Ms. Comstock to order the record.

A couple weeks later, I was summoned by the superintendent. Ms. Comstock, he told me, deemed "Hemingway Reading" inappropriate for teenagers.

I was nonplussed.

"She says it's pornographic."

"Pornographic? I can't believe it."

"She doesn't want the record in her library."

"You mean the *school* library, not *her* library."

"'An obscene waste of taxpayers' money,' were her words. She's going to destroy the record."

"Oh, not that," I said. "I'll buy it."

I left the superintendent's office and stopped by the treasurer's desk, where I forked over the money for the record.

"I'll call Ms. Comstock," said the treasurer. "I'll tell her you've paid for the record and will pick it up."

On the way to my classroom, I stopped by the library to retrieve "Hemingway Reading."

Ms. Comstock was all business. She retrieved the record from its holding cell on the banned bookshelf in her office. She placed it in a brown paper bag.

"I'm sorry about this, Ms. Comstock. I had no idea."

She raised her eyebrows, pursed her lips, and handed me the bag.

That evening after supper, after reading my daughter a picture book and putting her to bed, I placed "Hemingway Reading" on the turntable and sat down with a glass of wine. This would be pleasure, plus I was curious to learn what had offended Ms. Comstock. In the liner notes on the album I read that Hemingway had been wary of being recorded. I understood why. The author of the burly physique, of the fiction about bullfighting and boxing, fishing and war, of the "Hemingway Code Hero," had a voice squeaky as a parakeet's. I wasn't sure I wanted students to hear it either. I replaced disappointment with sweet irony and listened for what had offended Ms. Comstock.

Some minutes later my stereo speakers squawked with voiceless, bumping static. This was no parakeet; it was a Pterodactyl. I leapt from my chair, spilling wine, and rushed to the turntable. The needle slid wildly across the record. I lifted the LP off the spindle and brought it over to the light.

What the hell?! The fourth track on the LP was slick as an ice-covered pond. My mouth hung open. Not only did Ms. Comstock possess a black permanent marker. She also owned a single-edged razor blade. In her battle against impurity, she had scraped off every ridge and groove of track four of "Hemingway Reading." On the flip side, two more tracks had been scraped clean. At last, what Hemingway most feared had happened: the ol' misogynist had been emasculated by a woman.

24

menagerie

For its third year of publication I sought a more professional look-ing issue of *Menagerie*. Cost was a concern. My students had sold advertising space and designed ads. The graphics design/print shop at the county vocational school had quoted us a cut-rate price. That made professionally printing the magazine affordable. For their part, the vocational students would gain real-world experience in their trade. It was a sweet deal, but I was concerned. The print shop had had our magazine for over a month, and I hadn't heard a thing from them. Only a week and a half remained before graduating seniors finished the year. They were our main customers. I called the vocational school and asked for the print shop. The secretary connected me. A high school girl an-swered the telephone.

I told her who I was and why I was calling. Her voice caught, be-came guarded. She hemmed, she hawed. She cleared her throat and said, "You're supposed to call Mr. Bowdler."

"Who's he?" I asked. "What's he have to do with the magazine?"

"He's higher up," she blurted and hung up.

I called back and reached Mr. Bowdler.

His voice did not catch. He neither hemmed, nor hawed, nor cleared his throat. In an even, ominous tone he said, "There's a prob-lem with your magazine."

"Oh," I said.

"The four-letter words."

My voice caught. My breath quickened.

Mr. Bowdler read aloud from one story. "The intuition of that pas-sage," he said, "is sex."

The pedant in me rose up. "You mean *implication*, don't you?"

Mr. Bowdler brushed off my semantics lesson. "The intuition," he repeated, "is sex."

I felt my composure returning. "I'll come out and talk to you tomorrow."

"Fine," he said. "I'll see you then." His tone was a tad smug.

As I headed down the hall to my classroom, the seriousness of the situation confronted me: The writing and art of forty-five students in jeopardy of not being published after weeks of hard work. Scenes recently enacted were fresh in my memory: Joy, Becky, and Jeff poring over manuscripts, discussing the pieces, making editorial decisions, writing notes to authors, proofreading copy, the young writers listening carefully when we asked them to add detail to a passage or to dramatize a scene or to cut wordiness, then proudly bringing back their revised poems and stories; the four girls from the secretarial class who—in these days before computers—had spent hours typing and retyping the manuscripts until they had clean, finished copy ready for photographing in the print shop.

There's a problem with the magazine? Why hadn't they contacted me before now? Did they think the students' creative achievements meant so little that they could simply not follow through on our agreement and we wouldn't inquire? How gutless was that?

I wheeled around, headed back to the office, and called Mr. Bowdler.

"I'll be over at two," I told him.

My mind began a frantic circus act. I juggled the titles of scores of poems and stories. Which ones would Mr. Bowdler find offensive? Joy's "damn detention" and "oh shit"? Bobby's "my ass grounded" and "to hell with him"? Of course. Another story flashed into my mind: Kim's, titled "The Battle." Although it contained no swear words, the story revealed the naive, romantic expectations of a starry-eyed girl when she gets a date with Mr. Popular—the handsome, smooth-talking, all-around athlete who turns out to be conceited, spoiled, and sexually aggressive. No, I decided. Parents would applaud that story. Take a lesson, daughters!

The rest of the day my mind dwelt on the forthcoming meeting with Mr. Bowdler. I could talk to him, I told myself, explain to him why

the stories must contain those words, what the young writers were trying to accomplish through characterization and realistic dialog. There
were no bad words, I often told my five-year-old daughter. What mattered were the contexts in which words were used, and contexts meant
everything. I began to gain confidence.

That afternoon I sat in a chair with a loose armrest in Mr. Bowdler's
office. He sat forward, his arms folded on his big desk. "We at the vocational school cannot associate ourselves with a publication that contains four-letter words."

He snapped the cap onto his pen and leaned back in his chair. He
went on: "A girl in the print shop brought this matter to our attention.
A girl mind you."

It must have been that intuition working, I thought.

"I had punished her a week earlier for saying 'oh shit' to a teacher."

Oh, Jesus, I thought.

"She wanted to know why she had gotten a detention for swear-
ing, when we were going to print equally obscene words."

Mr. Bowdler picked up a manuscript and pointed out the word
damn in Kim's story, "The Battle." I'd forgotten about that "swear."

I sat forward. "Do you see the context the word is used in?"

Mr. Bowdler looked closely.

"The guy has tried to have his way with the girl," I said. "It's the
climax of the story. Every detail led to that moment."

Mr. Bowdler furrowed his brow.

"She stops his advances by kicking him in the shin. He could have
said a lot worse than *damn*."

Mr. Bowdler conceded my point.

"Do you see what the story is saying?" I asked. "The girl realizes how
naive she was and finally sees what a lout the guy is."

Mr. Bowdler sat back. "It doesn't matter what the story is saying,"
he said. "How can I justify punishing a student for saying 'oh shit' then
permit four-letter words to be published?"

"Isn't there a difference in the way the words are used?"

Mr. Bowdler told me a story about a boy who was kicked out of
the print shop program for intentionally misspelling a name on a job.
Five hundred business cards were sent to Harold Birch with the *r* of
his last name replaced with a *t*.

I suppressed a smart-assed remark about Harold Birch bitching and instead said, "Mr. Bowdler, you can't possibly tell me that we're talking about the same thing."

"Yes, we are. Your student and our students used obscene words to express themselves."

"It's not the same." I was growing impatient and angry. I had a keen sense of urgency. I was losing this battle. I sat forward. "One of your students disrespects a teacher. The other pulls a juvenile, low humor joke. You're saying that those are the same as my student who created a little world with words on paper to reveal a truth she's come to know about popularity, dating, and sex?"

I went on about teaching students to write honestly about what they know, about speaking "the rude truth," as Emerson put it.

"I see your point," said Mr. Bowdler. He shifted uncomfortably. "But what do I tell the girl who wants to know why we punished her then printed four-letter words?"

"Tell her the same thing I just told you."

Mr. Bowdler frowned, looked through the lower part of his bifocals, and shuffled some papers. "There is no difference," he said.

"There's no difference between reading a list of these words aloud and considering them in the context of a story?"

"No. These words should never be used. I wouldn't want my daughter writing a story like 'The Battle.'"

"My daughter is five, Mr. Bowdler. When she's seventeen, if she writes a story like 'The Battle,' I'll be proud."

"That's where we differ," said Mr. Bowdler. "The vocational school cannot be associated with a publication that contains four-letter words."

"Can the vocational school be associated with a quality creative arts magazine?"

"We were hoping, Mr. Romano, that you would delete all four-letter words and remove two of the stories so that we could proceed with publication."

"That's a radical stand," I said. "I've been telling my students to write honestly. I couldn't face them if I gave in to your demand."

"I wouldn't expect you to," he said.

Then why, I thought, did you ask?

I stood. "I wish you'd called when you saw the problem, Mr. Bowdler. I'm not sure we'll have time to print this now."

"You're welcome to the work that's been completed." He pointed to a fat folder on his desk. It contained all the negatives that had been shot from the clean manuscripts we provided.

I picked up the folder and left the vocational school, dejected, disillusioned, and angry.

Back at Edgewood, I told Phyllis what happened. She shook her head, astonished. Phyllis was the teacher who laughed heartily at Shakespeare's bawdy humor.

"I'm going to a professional printer. I don't know if we can cover the cost, though. The vocational school was printing it cheaply."

"First," said Phyllis, "you have to tell the principal what happened."

"He'll nix it. We'll never get it published."

"You have to tell the principal, Tom. You have to protect yourself."

I was more dejected than ever.

"Do you want me to go with you?" Phyllis asked.

I did.

We caught our principal just as he ended a phone call. Even at the end of the day, his gray suit and white shirt were unruffled. His tie was snugly in place. On one wall of his office hung that famous photograph by Eric Enstrom titled "Grace" that features an old man praying before a meager supper of soup and bread, a thick Bible he has been reading resting nearby on the table.

"We need your help with a problem," said Phyllis.

Our principal raised his eyebrows.

Quickly, I added, "Mr. Bowdler at the vocational school told me today that they wouldn't print *Menagerie* because it contained four-letter words."

His eyebrows remained aloft.

I mentioned the names of three of the students involved, all students he admired and respected, especially Kim, who was in the Honor Society and had been field commander of the marching band.

His eyebrows relaxed. Before we could say more, he was on the telephone. He put me in touch with Mr. Bruck, community member and printer by trade, a gentle man whose children had attended the local schools. Vicky, the Bruck's youngest of three children, had been my student just a year earlier. She was witty, intelligent, word-savvy, and compassionate. But she had not gone to college. She was home dying of cancer.

I was stunned by the principal's helpful response. When we were heading back to our classrooms, I asked Phyllis how on earth we had found success with the principal.

"We engaged him as an ally," she said. "We went to him with a request for help, not an ultimatum."

"He didn't even ask what the objectionable words were."

"He trusts us," said Phyllis.

I went to Mr. Bruck's that evening. We spread the negatives on the living room carpet. Mr. Bruck held each negative up to the light and clucked his tongue, pointing out where the work was shoddy. We discussed what needed to be done and the deadline we would need the printed copies by if the seniors were going to have a chance to buy them. All the while, Vicky—that dear, dear girl with so much personality, spunk, and wit—lay emaciated on the couch, dozing feverishly. Over the previous six months, I had brought her books to read, poems by Nikki Giovanni, James Agee's *A Death in the Family*, at her request. The last book she read was Dalton Trumbo's *Johnny Got His Gun*.

"Mr. Romano," she said—and here she extended her right hand, opening and closing her thin fingers as though grasping something tangible, "I like a book with some guts, one that isn't afraid to say something."

So did I. And I liked student writing with that same quality.

By working nights and one weekend, Mr. Bruck rescued our publication. *Menagerie* went on sale just in time.

Three days after that the principal caught me in the hall. His eyebrows were pushed together. "We're going to have to talk about the future of *Menagerie*."

Sweet Jesus, I thought. Would this never end?

"The students' writing," he said, "some of the words. . . ." Then he strode off on his principal's way. I returned to my classroom, and, as my students read, pulled out a yellow legal pad and dashed off an impassioned letter to the principal. I thanked him for his support of the magazine, then respectfully argued the case for context. Some girls, I wrote, were permitted to violate the dress code and wear skirts that barely covered the tops of their thighs, when, that is, they had donned their cheerleading uniforms. Some boys were permitted to square off and roughhouse each other, when, that is, they contained that violence within the context of a Friday night football game.

Before I left school that day, I stepped into the principal's empty office and dropped the letter on his desk. I heard nothing more from him.

Menagerie went on to be published for nearly twenty years.

25

soaring

I n 1980 a new superintendent began to lead the district, a recent Ph.D. from Miami University's Department of Educational Leadership: Roger Compton. He was young, intelligent, and personable. Roger brought a different management style to Edgewood. He believed in consultation and collaboration. He believed in strong relationships and building consensus. He sought faculty input and recruited their talents to help envision and plan a future. Communication was crucial to successful leadership, he thought. He established a district newsletter largely written by faculty members to disseminate information and publicize the good things happening in the school district. The newsletter went to every household and staff member.

A year prior to Roger's arrival, Gene Smith was promoted from vice principal to principal at the high school. Gene recognized the progressive work being done by teachers and encouraged us to pursue our professional passions. Gene was a big man—of height, of girth, of character. He cooked a delicious vegetable soup, and was a pro at clearing the way for teachers to do their good work. You went to him with a problem, he helped you solve it. You had good news, he reveled in it. You went to him with possibility, he made it actuality.

The English Department thrived in this atmosphere of openness and optimism. The sun had never shone brighter. Carolyn took an intensive journalism workshop one summer and revitalized the school newspaper. *Menagerie* became an annual ritual of spring. A new media specialist began stocking the library with young adult books. Phyllis' love of Shakespeare was contagious. Linda, Gary, Sue, and Mary joined her in producing several Shakespearian comedies. In her Bardic fervor,

Phyllis wrote a grant and brought in a Shakespeare impersonator for a week's residency.

Teaching writing flourished in the English Department and in the classrooms of a few scattered teachers throughout the school. Teachers used writing to deepen and widen students' learning. First semester of sophomore year evolved into a heterogeneously grouped writing and reading workshop. Later, in 1987, Nancie Atwell's *In the Middle* helped us manage the workshop so that it hummed right along. Our courses in introductory composition and creative writing fused into Writing I, a significant change that manifested our belief that the act of using language was a creative one, whether you were writing a poem or persuasive essay (or grocery list, for that matter). Purpose and audience might change, but using language was generative. We also knew that in much of the writing we liked the boundaries between genres were often blurred. Poems might contain dialog or swift lines of analysis. Fiction might contain incisive exposition. Essays could be funny and metaphorical with narrative used occasionally to make expository points. We used a smart, voiceful textbook to guide us: Ken Macrorie's *Writing to Be Read* (1976).

We were one enthusiastic department with group camaraderie and room for individuals to prosper. We were professionally vibrant. We knew our subjects and strove to learn more. Collectively, we were a force to be reckoned with. Administrators and curriculum directors trusted our lead in matters of language and literacy. It was a heady time.

And then in the early 1980s, we got a rocket boost akin to those old *Star Trek* episodes when the spaceship *Enterprise* moved from cruising speed to hyperspace. Stars became white streaks. Anything trailing was left behind. In the summer of 1980, the Ohio Writing Project held its first summer institute at Miami University. The project's founders were Mary Fuller, Max Morenberg, and Gil Storms.

Its second summer, I attended. The intensity, purposefulness, and collegiality of the course went beyond anything I'd experienced in education. It met four days a week, all day long, for five weeks. We studied writing. We taught each other what we knew. We wrote. We read seminal texts—among them, Peter Elbow's *Writing Without Teachers* (1973) and Janet Emig's *The Composing Processes of Twelfth Graders*

(1971). We read articles about language, writing, and teaching by other leading thinkers in the field: James Britton, Ann Berthoff, Don Murray, James Moffett, Don Graves, and Toby Fulwiler. We kept learning logs. We wrote poems, essays, stories, and a final culminating article that combined our teaching practice with theory and research.

Each morning of the institute began with a contemplative hour of writing. Twenty-five of us—teachers from elementary, middle, and high school—trickled in before our starting time, some driving from well over an hour away (that's how meteoric the Ohio Writing Project's reputation had become in just one year). We exchanged greetings, followed up on conversations and promises from the previous day. We each found our spots in the classroom and wrote. It was a blissful setting: bright morning classroom, cup of coffee within reach, my journal open, me writing with a favorite pen, hot in pursuit of ideas, explorations, and connections I was making from the reading, presentations, and conversations. Around me twenty-four passionate teachers wrote, too.

The three-day weekends allowed me time to dive further into writing and reading. Kathy, Mariana, and I lived in a conventional three-bedroom ranch house on a cement slab. Its one redeeming feature was a screened-in back porch that faced the rising sun—we used it from April through September. That's where I did my work. Summers in southwestern Ohio, however, can be brutal with heat and humidity. Sometimes even the porch was stifling.

Two of those long weekends when I wrote and revised a culminating article for the course, the heat and humidity pressed the back of my neck like a hot cloth. I'd begin to work in the morning, sitting on the porch writing on a yellow legal pad. Soon the paper became wet from my sweaty forearm. Perspiration slid down my bald head. I went to Miami, to air-conditioned Bachelor Hall. I took a thermos of coffee and everything I needed to write: pad, pens, note cards, books, and samples of student writing to illustrate my expository points. Bachelor Hall was virtually empty from Friday through Sunday. I climbed the stairs to our classroom, left the lights off, found my spot by a window, poured a cup of coffee, and wrote in the solitude, quiet, and coolness.

The Ohio Writing Project (OWP) showed me that I wasn't a lone wolf. As sustaining and energizing as our English Department at Edgewood was, the OWP connected me with a support system at Miami and with excellent teachers in the surrounding area. What we were doing at Edgewood was part of progressive thinking about teaching writing that was going on in pockets all over the country. There were teachers out there, in fact, making bolder moves than we were.

I spread word at Edgewood about OWP. Soon Phyllis and Carolyn went, then Linda, Sue, and Bonnie. Teaching at Edgewood became even headier.

I was an active OWP associate. I attended its meetings and conferences throughout the year. Part of Writing Project philosophy is that the best teacher of teachers are other teachers. A percentage of graduates from each summer institute went on to become writing consultants to area schools. An OWP consultant in 1981 was paid fifty dollars for a one-hour presentation plus any mileage or food expense incurred.

I took to this work on evenings and weekends, and sometimes during the school day if that could be arranged with my principal. It was gratifying to be recognized beyond my school for the work I was doing in teaching writing, for the professional expertise I was developing. The new learning excited me. The deeper knowledge and professional recognition boosted my confidence and made me a better teacher. I'll admit, too, that there is a goodly tablespoonful of the showman in me. I liked presenting my teaching strategies, theoretical underpinnings, and students' writing to other teachers. Some were as eager for learning as I was. Others were not. Some teachers did not like examining their practice of teaching writing, and they did not like some of the things I touted, like teaching grammar, usage, and mechanics as part of a process of writing, not as discrete knowledge studied apart from the craft itself. Some didn't like the notion that errors were not so much failures as possibilities for discovery and growth.

Years later when I was leaving Edgewood, Phyllis bought me a book as a going away present. Inside she used a theater metaphor to sum up that time we all taught together in that invigorating, collaborative atmosphere.

"We had a great run," Phyllis wrote.

We had indeed.

26

making plans

In late summer of 1983, Ann Koch saw me on the street in uptown Oxford. She had been a guidance counselor briefly at the high school and was now a dynamic principal at one of the grade schools in the district. One of Ann's teachers had become so interested in teaching writing, particularly in the work of Donald Graves, that Ann decided to investigate Graves herself. She had just returned from a workshop led by Graves and Lucy Calkins. Ann looked beatific, transformed. She projected a quiet, steadfast, almost devout commitment to children, learning, and literacy. A former elementary principal himself, Graves had been interested that Ann had come to the workshop. He and Ann had gone out for ice cream and talked at length. Graves told her about a new Ph.D. program in reading and writing instruction that was just getting off the ground where he taught at the University of New Hampshire.

I vaguely remembered Graves from an article of his we'd read during the Ohio Writing Project summer institute. I knew that his work was with children and writing. I didn't think that it had much to do with me, a high school English teacher. The effect he'd had on Ann, though, gave me pause. She had been profoundly moved by the encounter. His passion for writing and stories of children enchanted her. "You might want to think about that Ph.D. program, Tom. Graves would be wonderful to work with."

A doctoral program in reading and writing instruction? Could I do such a thing?

In October of that year, many of us classroom teachers who'd had OWP training attended a conference at Miami called "Sentence Combining and the Teaching of Writing." Scores of writing scholars and teachers had descended on Oxford. Keynote speakers were Peter Elbow, Bill Strong, and Don Murray. Murray was a key figure in the writing process movement from the 1960s and a present colleague of Graves at the University of New Hampshire. We listened to Elbow suggest the virtues of decombining sentences, saw him seized by ideas during his talk, thinking right on his feet in front of us. We listened to Murray discuss "Writing Badly to Write Well: Searching for the Instructive Line" (Murray 1985). In an image that has stayed with me for twenty-five years, Murray described his drafting process: ". . . lines searching for a meaning, a beagle running this way and that through my mind, nose to the ground, tail high, busy, busy, busy (Murray 1989, 38). Bill Strong's keynote was the last talk of the conference. Although I'd read his first sentence combining book for high school students years earlier, I didn't really know who Strong was, though he would become my colleague and friend eight years later when I took a job at Utah State University. In a substantive keynote, Strong synthesized Elbow's intellectual explorations and Murray's writerly insights, combining them with his own take on writing and teaching writing. Strong had experienced what we in the audience had experienced, and he made sense in a way that was both humorous and inspiring. During his talk, I scribbled in my journal:

> I've got to do it and it scares me—I've got to give myself the time
> to do it. I've got to quit teaching high school, at least for a while,
> and voyage out in my rickety boat. Tom, ever since early college
> when you discovered you weren't as smart as you thought you
> were (after the shock of realizing that), you made yourself go with
> your best then be content—Do it now.

So impassioned was I after that stimulating conference that I composed a letter to Donald Graves, though I had never met him. I inquired about the Ph.D. program that Ann had told me about. Here is the last paragraph of the letter:

> Until three weeks ago I considered my life settled and my niche
> at Edgewood High School secure. I was content. Now I'm afire.
> Uproot, let go, voyage out, reach for something I'm not sure I can

grasp. My feelings are akin to the thrill and fear I felt as a boy when we ventured from our warm houses on Halloween night. In our paper bags was plenty of shucked corn, in our pockets were thick bars of Ivory soap, in our hearts was the sweet anxiety of great expectation.

I bought Graves' book, *Writing: Teachers and Children at Work* (1983). In the spring of 1984, Graves visited Miami University for three days, a joint venture sponsored by the departments of English and Teacher Education. I attended all Graves' sessions in the late afternoon and evening. Ann introduced me to Graves, and we three went for a glass of wine. Graves told me he expected the new Ph.D. program to be officially approved in a matter of weeks. As I sat at the table, fingering the stem of a wine glass, Graves said from memory Richard Wilbur's moving poem, "The Writer." I took that as a good omen. Maybe I was being wished "lucky passage."

A few weeks later, I got word that the doctoral program was approved. The deadline for applying was tight and required significant writing on the application. One question asked applicants to write about three books that had influenced them. It was a fat pitch that invited a full swing. I wrote about Justin Kaplan's *Walt Whitman: A Life* (1980), George Gabori's *When Evils Were Most Free* (1981), and Graves' book, *Writing: Teachers and Children at Work* (1983). (I knew I risked appearing to suck up with that choice, but I'd finished it the day before Graves arrived at Miami. I easily saw how his work with children applied to my work with teenagers.)

For one session during his Miami visit, Graves met with eight third graders seated around a table. With these children he'd never met before, Graves went from talking with them about books they had read to passing out pencils and paper and leading them into writing about what they knew. The whole time, sixty of us teachers sat along the perimeter of the room watching. It was a synthesizing experience for me. My reading of Graves' book—and of Murray's *Write to Learn* (1984) that spring—my own experience as a writer, the powerful scene of teaching and learning enacted in the center of the room . . . all these came together in a torrent of language I jotted on the program sheet to capture the image I witnessed. Over the next few weeks, I worked the raw words into a poem that I sent off to *Language Arts* (Romano 1985, 142):

Eight Children Teach Donald Graves

Nine pencils break the surface of awareness,
jutting into the air,
slanted back like
yellow, orange tipped shark fins,
entering chartless white,
exploring hazy depths.

Nine voices search a scent,
suddenly lurch,
lose the line,
pause,
pick it up again
and move from
cloudy, roiling waters
of new thought
through warm currents of reception,
straits of questioning,
and tidal imbalances
to a clear, precise
sea of meaning.

I sent in my application to the Ph.D. program. In June I was accepted.

I applied for and received a year's leave at Edgewood High School, just in case graduate school didn't work out. We put our house of three years on the market. Not even an offer. We tried renting it. No takers. In fact, the husband of one couple who considered it was such an abrasive boor that we were loath to rent it to anyone.

Kathy thought I should go to UNH myself, at least that first year. She and Mariana would stay in Ohio, she continuing to work her nursing job in the recovery room at the local hospital, Mariana attending eighth grade. I thought of Ma Joad in the *Grapes of Wrath*: "Don't break up the family, Tommy." But another literary voice fueled my fire to reach for something I wasn't sure I could grasp. "I celebrate myself and sing myself," Walt Whitman said to me.

Before Labor Day I drove a thousand miles to another part of the country, where autumn was fiery and chocolate candy sprinkles over ice cream were called jimmies, where the great Atlantic Ocean was fifteen minutes away, and where *writer* became *writah*.

At UNH I moved into Babcock Hall, the graduate school dormitory on campus. My room was six feet by twelve feet and contained a single bed, a closet, two large drawers, and a desk and bookshelf built into the wall. I set up a card table at the foot of my bed to hold my portable Smith Corona typewriter and later that year my first computer, a PC Junior. Out my narrow window across a sandy volleyball court was the Whittemore School of Business & Economics in McConnell Hall, which many of the graduate students in the dorm attended. Every few weeks I flew back to Ohio on People's Airlines, God bless it. No frills, no meals, ticketing on board at your seat. Seventy-five dollars one way between Columbus and Boston. I could buy a can of beer for a dollar.

After I'd been accepted into the program that summer, Jane Hansen called to offer me my choice of assistantships at UNH: I could teach one section of first-year composition in the English department or I could work as a research assistant on the project that she and Graves were conducting at Mast Way Elementary School in Lee, New Hampshire. She gave me time to think about it. I asked OWP co-director, Max Morenberg, which assistantship he thought I should choose.

"Are you out of your mind?" Max said. Although there were phonetic similarities between *Max* and *tact*, the words had little in common with each other. "If you want to teach college freshmen to write, you can do that at Miami. You don't have to go to New Hampshire. My God, Tom! You've got a chance to work with Don Graves! Don't blow it!"

I didn't. I called Jane and told her I wanted to work on the research project.

4

UNH

27

giants

I spent four mornings each week in Jan Roberts' third-grade classroom at Mast Way School in Lee, New Hampshire. My job was to gather qualitative data on the teacher and the children. We sought to discover how teachers changed and grew, how their own literacy and professional development affected their teaching choices. We also sought to find out how children learned to read and write. There were five of us on the university research team: Don Graves worked with second-grade teacher Leslie Funkhouser, Jane Hansen with fourth-grade teacher Phyllis Kinsey, Ruth Hubbard—a paid research assistant—with first-grade teacher Pat McClure, and graduate assistant Lorri Neilsen with librarian Marcia Taft. In addition to researching in Jan's classroom, I—along with Ruth and Lorri—assisted university videographer Jim Whitney as he documented the work of the children and teachers.

My experience with Jan and the children was surely, if not quickly, leading me to divest myself of elitist notions of literacy. There was, I discovered, a great deal to learn from eight-year-olds and their teacher, if only I could keep at bay my uninformed assumptions about what children could do. Jan ran her literacy block in the morning as workshops. In the forty-five-minute writing workshop, children wrote pieces about topics they were passionate about, just as authors did. Jan kept track of their progress and nudged them along through individual conferences. The forty-five-minute reading workshop that followed ran in much the same way. Jan was an aficionado of children's literature, and the library was packed with it. Children chose their own books, wrote about them in reading logs, and conferred with Jan about their reading. Later in the year when Jan discovered how much she and four students dominated classroom discussion, she organized students into peer groups so more of them would have a chance to talk about their reading and writing. Our research method was not hands off. We didn't sit back and watch literate life unfold. We asked questions, conducted interviews, and taught and learned right along with the children. I took pages and pages of notes, soon developing a callous on my right forefinger.

Each Friday the university research team met for two hours. We discussed our research observations, related triumphs and failures, solved problems, and planned videotaping sessions and visits to each other's classrooms. We five also were a writing group, much like the ones Peter Elbow described in *Writing Without Teachers* (1973). We each brought a piece we had written to the meeting, a narrative Don and Jane called it, a few pages in which we captured the human experience of learning to read and write and teach. Over the course of the two hours, we each read aloud our writing to the others.

Oh, did I ever feel the pressure that first meeting! Don Graves a member of my writing group? Don Graves who had done more than anyone at that time to change the way children learned to write, whose first book had been a best-seller among literacy teachers. And if I'd known what fine writers and thinkers Jane, Ruth, and Lorri were, I might have suffered such feelings of inadequacy that I would never have written a word. Jane was an avid writer and would become one of the great literacy leaders in the land. Lorri, from Halifax, had a writer's sensibility and a first-rate linguistic intelligence. Her third book, *Knowing Her Place* (1998), won the CEE Richard Meade Award in 1999. Ruth would go on to write more than a dozen books over the years about literacy education and research. Hers are some of the smartest, most readable books in the profession.

I didn't take the narratives lightly. I knew the writing process I had to go through to get to gold. After my first day of research, I went to the Dimond Library and wrote a draft in longhand on a yellow legal pad. I went through my usual routine of revising the draft, typing a copy, revising that, typing another clean copy, and maybe revising that draft, too. For that first narrative I wrote about one of the third-grade boys who'd had a difficult time adjusting to the first day of school. I nailed the story.

It was hard not to write well, given our dynamic subject matter and the context of that writing group. Unlike some writing groups in college that were red in tooth and claw, there was no need to be affrighted of this group of talented writers and gifted teachers. Their narratives each week were insightful, vivid, full of children's voices, and swiftly analytical. We paced each other, I think. Through our narratives (and sometimes poems, one-act plays, and even a blues song once) we showed each other possibilities.

Over the course of the year, we each wrote two dozen narratives. I learned to write fast. I still began the writing, however, early enough so I had time to draft, let it sit a day, then engage in at least one revision session before printing a final copy. I heard poet laureate Billy Collins say once that students think revision is what you do after the party. Revision, in fact, is the party. Kim Stafford says that "revision happens best when it can have the same fervency as first writing." He calls this "the second genius" (Stafford 2003, 36).

I was never at a loss for what to write about. The subject matter was so rich: twenty-four eight-year-olds learning to be print literate with a lot of choice about what they read and wrote. Of all my experiences at UNH that year, my work with the children and Jan, and the writing associated with it, remain my biggest learning, my most fulfilling writing. Here are two pieces from my Mast Way narratives, two sketches of very different boys on very different literacy roads. I learned from them both:

The Ideal Solution

I came by third grader Danny's desk and asked him how the piece about his rabbit was progressing. He was stuck, he said. He'd added information his peer group had inquired about. Now he didn't know where to go. That was his dilemma, he thought, but before he could move on that problem, another supplanted it when I asked him to read to me what he'd written. The last two sentences read, "We pot my rabbit in a caige in our barn. We feed my rabbit rabbit pelets and carits."

"Ooops," said Danny. "Something wrong there."

"What?"

"Rabbit rabbit."

"What's wrong with that?"

"Doesn't sound right."

"What can you do about it?"

"I don't know—change punctuation?"

"Which one?"

"A question mark."

Danny wrote in a question mark. I read him how that convention made the passage read: "We feed my rabbit? Rabbit pelits and carits."

"Nope," said Danny. He erased the question mark, replacing it first with a comma, then a period, and finally an exclamation point. After each insertion, he read the sentence aloud. None of the punctuation marks solved the problem. "Nope . . . nope . . . nope."

He sat back. "I don't know what to do."

"So you've discovered that the problem isn't with punctuation?"

He looked at me as though I were completely lame.

I didn't let that bother me. I was used to saying dumb things to the children. One boy, in fact, always mispronounced my name, calling me "Mr. Morono." At least, I think he was mispronouncing my name. I persisted, "If punctuation won't help, Danny, then what's the problem with?"

"I don't . . . I know! I'll get rid of the second *rabbit*!"

He did, then read, "We feed my rabbit pelets and carits." He was pleased. Problem solved.

"What are these pellets anyway?" I asked.

"Rabbit food."

"It's especially for rabbits?"

"Yeah, there's chicken pellets, too." Danny frowned. "I gotta use rabbit pellets," he moaned, "or the reader won't know what kind of pellets my rabbit is eating." He rewrote the troublesome word.

"What can you do?" I asked.

"I don't know."

"If you were willing to get rid of the second *rabbit*, why not get rid of the first?"

Danny looked puzzled.

"Is there another word you could use for *rabbit*?"

"Nope. It's my rabbit."

Use a pronoun, I thought to myself. Call "my rabbit" him—the ideal solution.

"Bunny!" cried Danny. "We feed my bunny rabbit pellets. I can say that, can't I? They call rabbits bunnies sometimes."

"Yes, they do."

Danny completed the change. I congratulated him on his successful revision. Then I reflected on his problem-solving process: rereading aloud so he could use his developing ear, imbalance perceived, new imbalance discovered, no solution, four failures in the wrong ballpark, one solution that worked temporarily but created a new problem. And finally a solution he could live with. He hadn't come up with the obvious solution, the one I had thought of from the beginning—to use a pronoun to replace the noun. Instead, Danny had come up with a better solution—the ideal solution—his own.

I was learning how to urge along students' thinking. Instead of offering them answers like dog yummies, I was using questions to discover how they perceived their learning and to lead them to their own cognitive grappling, a surer move toward significant learning than dispensing correct answers to children. I found that when I looked deep inside and remained open and curious, the surprises came flying.

The Poet Within

Not until late February did I suspect that third grader Kenneth was a poet. Last October when he had explained to me that the wool of his lambs was two different colors because the tips sometimes got burned by the sun, I thought he was perceptive, but I did not think he was a poet. Too much about him threw me off.

When he spoke, for example, he often needed half a dozen false starts before the first sentence got rolling. The retainer he wore slurred his speech, as though he held too much saliva in his mouth. Throughout most of September Kenneth appeared to bide his time, accomplishing little. And then for one solid month he missed school while he traveled to California with his mother. Kenneth became a dark spot in my data gathering. Now, in late February, he blazed brightly. In every subject he excelled. And I believed he was a poet.

A week earlier he had read aloud to the class his piece in progress, "The Case of the Falling Man." I was struck by some of the words he used: *silhouette*, *sharp cry*, and *sprinted*. None of the children mentioned these words when they talked about the piece in group share. They had plenty of comments and questions, though, about the story of twelve-year-old Peter who thought he saw a man fall over the edge of the Grand Canyon. Kenneth's word choice, though, had certainly made me pay attention.

Two days later I walked by Kenneth's desk as he finished a reading log entry. The title of the book he was reading prompted me to stoop beside him.

"What made you choose this?" I asked.

"I—uh—well—it—I like Christmas and the pictures are really interesting."

"The author was a famous poet, you know."

"I didn't know that."

"May I read what you wrote about it?"

He assented and pushed the reading log my way. I read his response to *A Child's Christmas in Wales* by Dylan Thomas.

"Kenneth, you quoted from the book, '. . . and cats in their fur-abouts watched the fires.' Why do you like that?"

"I like cats and I like fires. Also, you get a lot of information from one little phrase."

"You seem to like words."

Kenneth nodded.

"How come you like them so much?"

"I think I inherited a love of words from my grandfather," he said. "And he must have inherited it from my great grandfather 'cause he loved words, too."

"How do you know they loved words?"

"They played with words a lot. They made up new words."

"How exactly did they play with them?"

"Like my brother and I made up the word *blugurt*."

"*Blugurt*?"

"We took blueberry yogurt and made it sort of a contraction."

"You know, Kenneth, the other day I noticed you used the words *sprinted* and *sharp cry* in your story. I thought they were quite effective. You're really careful about the words you pick when you write."

"I try to make one word explain a lot of words so I won't have to say, 'a high-pitched loud cry.' I just say, 'sharp cry.' And *sprinted* would be 'a short distance.' Instead of saying, 'He ran a short distance,' I say, 'He sprinted.' "

"Do you ever read over what you've written and see a place where you could get rid of three words by using one?"

"Well," Kenneth said, "sometimes you want to have it long. Sometimes the words make more sense when you leave it longer."

"Do you ever write poetry?"

"I did once," he said. "The poem that's hanging out in the hall. It's titled 'Beautiful Day in Switzerland.' "

"Show it to me, will you?"

Kenneth led me into the hall to the spot where a large picture mounted on yellow construction paper hung on the wall. The assignment from the art teacher had been to create a snow scene with poster paints and outline the figures with crayon. The painting was to show perspective, with objects and figures in the foreground larger than those in the background. Kenneth had drawn a man chopping wood. Behind him was an expanse of snow that led to a mountain range. At the base of the mountains, a train chugged along, its cars white, green, and red. Stapled to the bottom of the painting was a sheet of paper with his poem on it. Kenneth read to me in his slurred speech. When he finished, I asked why he had chosen this topic.

"I like the Swiss Alps. The reason I thought of Switzerland," he added, "is because I read *Banner in the Sky* and that takes place in Switzerland."

Kenneth and I went back into the classroom.

"So what makes 'Beautiful Day in Switzerland' a poem?"

"It sort of has a rhythm."

"Now, let me get this straight," I said. "You painted the picture in art class and then the art teacher had you write a poem to it."

"No, Mrs. Roberts did. She said if we wanted to, we could write something to go with our painting."

"It didn't have to be a poem?"

"No."

"What made you decide to write a poem?"

"I didn't want to write something that didn't have rhythm."

"Do you ever read poems?"

"Yeah, I've memorized part of 'Tyger, Tyger.' It goes,

> Tyger, Tyger, burning bright
> In the forests of the night
> What immortal hand or eye
> Could frame thy fearful symmetry?"

My goodness, I thought. William Blake. I was a sophomore in college before I was introduced to his poetry. "Where did you catch on to that poem?" I asked.

"My brother had to memorize it for school. He's in sixth. I just happened to hear him while he was practicing, and I learned part of it. There's more."

I thanked Kenneth for the talk, gathered my things, and left the room. I crossed the hall and stood in front of his painting and poem that was almost lost amid the other pieces of student art. It took a close look to discern any difference between Kenneth's and the others, but difference there surely was.

And then I spoke the words of his poem:

Beautiful Day in Switzerland

> A Swiss woodcutter with
> The snowcapped Alps behind,
> And the three cars of a
> train, and the big black

engine, puffing black
smoke, and the big, blue,
beautiful Swiss winter sky.

Imagery, alliteration, assonance, and try saying those last
seven words without getting caught up in the sound and rhythm
of them. Kenneth, Kenneth, burning bright . . . what immortal
hand or eye . . . ?

28

meltdown

That first semester at UNH had been the most productive months of reading and writing I'd ever spent. In addition to the research at Mast Way, I'd taken three courses: Teaching Reading in Secondary Schools, Children's Literature, and Introduction to Teaching Writing, this course with Don Graves. The reading and writing had stretched me to the limit. In addition to the weekly narratives I wrote for the Mast Way research, the Children's Lit class required a great deal of reading too, wonderful reading of countless genres and scores of books, but hours and hours of reading nevertheless. I took the ten writing assignments attached to these books seriously, too, and made them my own. I dug right in so requirements wouldn't pile up at the end.

I wrote faster than I ever had before, still lived healthily in revision, but accelerated my writing process. There was no time for writer's block. As my one physical outlet I swam laps four or five times a week at the university pool. My life was streamlined: breakfast at the dining hall, research at Mast Way, reading, writing, swimming, reading, writing, class, reading, writing, supper, readingwritingreadingwritingreadingwriting. Stress mounted. For Children's Literature, I read a picture book of the myth of Sisyphus, that knave of Greek mythology who was condemned by the Gods to roll a boulder up a steep hill. When he reached the summit, Sisyphus watched in horror as the boulder rolled back down the hill. He trudged down to the boulder and began rolling it uphill again, always with the same results. Unlike the toil of Sisyphus, my work was fulfilling. I wasn't rolling the same boulder continually over the same ground. Even so, the myth made me squirm. My work seemed endless. Every assignment that needed to get done got done. On time and with as much quality as I could muster. I'd take a breath, then put my shoulder to the next assignment.

In December, a few days before Christmas, the evening of my last exam, I was tranquil. All but this last hurdle was left in the semester. Behind me were hundreds of thousands of words I had read and written. I'd prepared as much as I could for the exam. I was laid back, confident, ready to show what I knew one more time then fly home to my wife and daughter in Ohio. A teacher from Maine surprised us that evening by baking Irish Soda Bread. Penny and I had been the only experienced teachers in the class, along with twenty young women in the UNH master's degree/teacher certification program. Penny brought an extra loaf of soda bread for me. It was wrapped in foil, still warm, delicious.

The next morning about five, amid a snowstorm, I loaded my massive, unwheeled suitcase onto a grocery cart I found outside Babcock and pushed it through deep snow a few sloping blocks to the bus stop in Durham. The way was bumpy and bucking, every curb and obstacle covered by the snow—this trek was actually closer to the physical labor of Sisyphus than my reading and writing. I was sweating profusely when I boarded the bus for the hour and a half ride to Logan Airport in Boston. I was weary and satisfied, sobered, too, by the experience of doctoral work. I had a keen sense of accomplishment.

I also had a nervous twitch in my left eye. Every so often the eyelid fluttered madly for a few seconds. I was fifteen pounds lighter than four months earlier, my weight dropping to 157 in early December, less than I'd weighed as a high school senior. I harbored a vague sense of dread in anticipation of the following semester when I would take three more classes, one of them a seminar in teaching reading. Although there were only two classes required in the program, there was a tacit understanding that graduate students would take this reading seminar and, also, in a future semester, a statistics course—"So you'll know how to read quantitative research, not that you'll have to conduct it, of course."

The break between semesters sped by. During it, I read books that were on the Ph.D. reading list. I wrote a semester report on the research I'd done at Mast Way. My dread increased as the break reached its end.

In late January I was back at UNH. One of the first things I did was travel to Mast Way and reunite with Jan and the children. The three

courses I took that semester were a seminar in writing research with
Graves, a seminar in composition with Murray, and the seminar in
teaching reading—a course for which I felt totally unprepared. I was
in a fragile state, but once more ready to jump into the breach and give
my all as I had done the previous semester. Dig that ditch with a fury.

The first night of the reading seminar was congenial enough, though
the professor's language was alien to me. I found the concepts and jar-
gon clinical, esoteric, and beyond my ken. This world of teaching reading was not my world of literature and writing. I didn't live in it. I didn't
want to learn to live in it. Everyone sitting around that seminar table
but me seemed to know about teaching reading. The professor said that
initially he would be presenting a lot, until we had gathered enough
knowledge about teaching reading to contribute productively to the
seminar. We would learn just enough statistics, he said, to understand
the research we'd be reading and to complete assignments that to me
looked complex and lengthy. I felt strapped to my chair, as though
aboard an airplane speeding toward a destination I did not want to go.
The other passengers were eager for the trip. Not me. I wanted off. I
wanted to somehow zig or zag.

The next day on campus on my way to Morrill Hall, I saw Don
Graves, walking purposefully in my direction.

"Can we have a conference?" I asked.

"Let's make it next week," he said. "Give me a call."

He stepped by me and we headed in opposite directions.

"Tom!" Don called. I turned around. He pointed at me. "Can you
be at the house at four?"

"Yes," I said.

"See you then." He swiveled and hurried away.

At four I sat in Don's home office, a spacious room where he could
spread out data and do his writing, a place that accommodated a dozen
people on folding chairs for meetings and seminars. Don was usually
upbeat, positive, quick to note irony, quick to make and recognize
humor. He wasn't light and upbeat now. He sat across from me looking serious, listening.

I told him that I couldn't finish the doctoral program, that I didn't
want to live the life I saw I would have to live in order to stay on top.
I didn't want to be a traditional reading teacher and that seemed to be
where the program was directing me.

My voice quavered. I barely had breath to give sound to my words. Don listened and watched. I was butter in a microwave oven, melting before his eyes.

"I was a first-rate high school teacher," I said. Tears sprang to my eyes. "I don't want to be a second-rate college teacher." My voice caught. I swallowed. "I can't keep up this pace."

I breathed deeply, felt myself settling down, gaining self-control. It was good to speak my anxieties.

Don talked about my working style. He thought I was a refiner, too much for my own good, that the worst thing anybody could say about my work was that it was sloppy.

"You don't pick spots to excel in," Don said. "You don't slough off too well. You go at everything full tilt."

He was right. The only way I knew was all out. I was a slow reader, a ponderous learner, more comfortable in details than in big vision. But Don was also wrong about something. The worst thing anyone could say about my work, I believed, was that it lacked substance, was intellectually empty.

"What's the bottom line?" Don asked.

His tone surprised me. It seemed almost aggressive. I was puzzled. "I don't understand?"

"Are you going home tomorrow?"

"I wouldn't do that," I said. "The research at Mast Way means too much. I agreed to come to UNH for the year. I'm dropping the reading seminar, but I'm staying until the end of the semester."

Don nodded. "Regardless of your career decision," he said, "the only way we will lose touch is if you choose to."

Before I left that evening, I thanked Don for agreeing to meet with me when we'd encountered each other on campus.

"There was something in your face," Don said. "I almost missed it."

With my decision to drop the reading seminar and leave the program, my stress level decreased. I gained equanimity. I called my high school principal at Edgewood and told him I would return in the fall. I concentrated on doing good work at Mast Way and in the two classes I carried. In Graves' seminar, I learned further qualitative research methods, designed and carried out a project in which I investigated who did most of the talking in Jan's classroom. In Murray's seminar I examined the connections between writing and film making, wrote a one-pager each week to report my learning, and joined Lorri Neilsen in writing a collaborative article to Murray's enthusiasm.

I'd never been more at peace with a big decision. I knew it was right. The eye-twitching stopped. My weight stabilized. The semester was fulfilling. And before I left UNH in May 1985, one more thing happened that altered the course of my life.

29

final assignment

D on Graves stepped over to the writing process lab, where I was working. "Tom," he said, "there's someone I want you to meet." He took me to his office and introduced me to Philippa Stratton, his editor at Heinemann. She was London born, white-haired, and cordial. She had the most alert eyes I'd ever seen. Her demeanor, the sound and rhythm of her British accent, her very presence communicated optimism and possibility.

Philippa extended her hand and said, "Would you like to write a book about teaching writing in high school?"

Earlier, Philippa had told Don that Heinemann had the teaching of writing in elementary school covered pretty well, but it needed a book about teaching writing for high school teachers.

"I know the guy who can write that book," Don told her. He handed Philippa one of my Mast Way narratives.

"Write a book?" I said to Philippa. "Oh, no, I couldn't possibly write a book."

"No?"

"No. I'm . . . I'd be overwhelmed. I've written articles, but a book. . . ."

"Don't think of it as a book," said Philippa. "Think of writing seven articles."

"It's still a book. I don't know."

"Think it over," she said. "Then get in touch."

I went back to Babcock that day with *book* on my mind. Not Book Graves or Book Murray. I was thinking Book Romano. Was that possible? No. Definitely not. During the night, however, I leapt from bed, snapped on the desk light, and wrote furiously for a few minutes, jotting down topics for possible chapters that had suddenly surfaced in my mind. What did I have to say about teaching writing to high school teachers? Plenty, I was coming to realize. Over the next two weeks, I added ideas to my list. My confidence grew. I called Philippa and told her I'd write the book.

"Oh, marvelous," she said. "I'm so glad. Now, we'll need to get an idea what your book will be like. Could you send me a prospectus?"

I agreed, then immediately searched for the book prospectus that Don Murray had given us earlier in the semester, a handout I filed but knew I would never look at again. I also talked to Graves about writing a prospectus.

"Make it clear and simple," he said. "Let your voice come through. That's what Philippa liked when she read your narrative."

For three weeks ideas percolated. I entertained them all, rejected nothing. I was so afraid I wouldn't have enough material for a book. I never trusted memory. When an idea came, I jotted it down, which more than once compelled me to rise from bed. A book. By me. My own book. Really?

One weekend I wrote and revised a one-page description of the book I imagined and the titles of sixteen possible chapters, each annotated with a sentence or two. I took the draft to Graves for a conference. I needed a companion for my words. I hoped he'd go over what I'd written line by line, but, of course, that wasn't Don's style. He first received my writing, telling me the content of it that he had under-

stood. Then he asked me questions that got me talking about teaching writing. I confessed that I didn't know if I could write full chapters about some of the things I'd proposed.

"You should see my first prospectus! The book I wrote was a good deal different from the book I imagined I'd write. The prospectus," Don said, "is to get Heinemann to say 'yes.'"

I revised the prospectus one more time and sent it off.

Philippa called and told me it looked good. I was delighted. Then she told me she would send the prospectus out for critique. Depending on the nature of that response, they at Heinemann would decide whether to proceed with the project.

Whether to proceed? I'd thought that sending my prospectus to Heinemann would seal the deal. But Heinemann wanted to see how my writing and ideas would be received by professionals in the field. The process of producing a book, I was learning, was divided into steps, at least in my case.

In three weeks the critique of my prospectus came back. Steve Zemelman of the Illinois Writing Project had done the responding, yet another companion for my words. Zemelman made me want to write. He wrote, "The images bursting out in many spots in the proposal show Romano's ability to present ideas vividly, to write well himself, and to engage high school teachers, who will, after all, be choosy, demanding readers."

Zemelman followed that with two-and-a-half, single-spaced pages in which he mentioned "additional issues, strengthenings, and shifts" I might consider.

Philippa was pleased with his response. We discussed the prospectus' strengths, weaknesses, and omissions—like evaluation. Zemelman noted that I might want to say something about evaluation since teachers were keenly interested in that.

Now, I thought, I was ready to begin writing the book.

"We'd like to see two trial chapters," Philippa said. "We'll send those to readers who would likely read a book like yours. From there we'll decide whether to proceed with drawing up a contract."

Trial chapters? And again, "Whether to proceed"?

"Let's see," said Philippa. "What would be reasonable? Could you get me the chapters by mid-August?"

It was almost June. I'd have two and a half months. Before I wrote a word, however, I went to the gold mine I had produced in Graves' two courses. He'd had us keep learning journals. In them I'd written hundreds of pages of handwritten, informal prose. I'd written about the required readings and research, but I'd also made the journal my own and permitted myself unrestrained exploration of any topic of writing, reading, and teaching I wandered into. I roamed freely over my thirteen years of high school teaching.

My journals were replete with ideas, metaphors, anecdotes, connections I was newly making, and my evolving educational philosophy. In that unpressured journal, I had written phrases, lines, sometimes entire paragraphs so well-articulated in the heat of writing fast that I lifted them out and used them in the book. I numbered the pages in my journals, then reread them, using note cards to write down particular information I had written about and where I could find it. Then I matched the cards with chapters I proposed to write. Some ideas in my prospectus fell away. Other ideas gained added importance. And best of all, new ideas emerged.

I wrote three trial chapters: one titled "Please Write" and two about "Writing Amid Literature." "Please Write" was about the benefits that accrue when a writing teacher actually writes. It was critical, I believed, that students know their teacher not just as an assigner of writing, but as a writer, as someone practicing what she teaches.

I wrote the chapters the best I could, then sent the forty, double-spaced pages to Carolyn Smith, my colleague at Edgewood, whom I would be joining once again in August. Carolyn was yet another companion for my words. She sent the manuscripts back to me with comments in the margins and "goods" in places that particularly struck her. On one manuscript she wrote, "Tom—this builds, circles, remembers, and builds again—good points." Amid the positive comments, she asked four specific questions that helped me to revise.

By the mid-August deadline, I sent the chapters to Heinemann. A month later I received responses from two readers. One of them was a middle school teacher from Boothbay Harbor, Maine, who was fast gaining a reputation as a premiere writing teacher. She was, in fact, writing a book of her own about teaching writing and reading.

"I was happy to review these three chapters," Nancie Atwell wrote. "Tom Romano writes so well, and his style is his own. There's a genuine voice at work here—teacher, scholar, poet and storyteller combined. His stuff is eminently readable; it's also fun to read."

Then she followed with specific responses, sometimes praising, sometimes helping me with honest statements such as, "I enjoyed the two 'Writing Amid Literature' chapters, but I think these two are in need of some cutting and untangling." And then she told precisely where and how they'd become tangled for her.

I was clearly seeing that writing a book was a collaborative process. Five months earlier, I thought I'd hole up, write the manuscript, and send it to Heinemann. I'd be a lone wolf, licking my literacy chops, the one solely responsible for keeping the scent of my writing strong. But lone wolves, I realized, were the exception. Wolves by nature were social. Wolves were at their best when they relied on each other. So it was with writers and those in their world: editors, readers, fellow writers, companions all.

On the strength of the chapter reviews, Heinemann issued me a contract. I was to deliver the completed manuscript one year later— August of 1986. They would pay me a one thousand dollar advance. I signed the contract and told Heinemann to keep the money. I still wasn't convinced I could write the book. Then school started.

5
Reentry

30

reentry

Returning to Edgewood High School was culture shock. Even though the research work at Mast Way had kept me close to students' writing, reading, and learning, those students were little ones. I hadn't been around teenagers and the values in an American high school in more than a year.

My reentry, though, promised to be smooth: Roger Compton was still superintendent, and still progressive, fair, and open-minded. Gene Smith was still principal. He was glad to have me back. The English Department was running full steam ahead. Phyllis had advised *Menagerie* the year I was gone and led it to its twelfth year of publication. I returned to my same schedule that fall: two classes of sophomore reading and writing workshop, three classes of film communication, and one writing class for juniors and seniors. I was bursting with ideas to implement.

The culture shock came in two ways:

A new head football coach had arrived the year I was absent. He prided himself on motivating players and generating team spirit. The rift in school between athletes and nonathletes was greater than ever. In August the local newspaper ran two half-page photographs of the team. One was titled "Gangsta Offense" and featured the boys dressed like 1930s hoodlums in pinstriped suits, toting machine guns. The other photo was titled "Rambo Defense." Head bandannas, ripped T-shirts, and large hunting knives were the motifs. In both photos the boys scowled. They were all business, and the business, their poses announced, was kicking ass.

It got worse. The coach had founded a new organization called Guardian Angels. Teenage girls only. They had to exude school spirit. They had to want to support and care for the gangstas and Rambo wannabes. They were all physically attractive. Throughout game week each angel "guarded" a player, bringing him surprise gifts, fetching him lunch items from the cafeteria, writing and delivering supportive, bolstering notes throughout the day. The angels made the players feel special, admired, and privileged because of their hard work, dedication, and sacrifice on the football field. On Thursday evenings, the guardian angels decorated the lockers of the football players so that on Friday morning—on game day—they would be surprised and inspired by what they found. At each week's pep rally, the guardian angels wore their special player's football jersey. There were so many guardian angels that some players had two girls assigned to him, two girls to pamper, praise, and worship him.

I wanted to puke. I wasn't offended; I was pissed. I complained of the sexual stereotyping. Most faculty shrugged. Most students rolled their eyes or looked amazed that I could think such a thing. I was making much ado about nothing. People enjoyed the guardian angels: the players, the parents, especially the girls. My daughter was fourteen then. Although she went to another high school, I was galled by the idea that a public school would sanction such gender stereotyping, would channel its bright, teenage girls into roles of subservient, self-effacing, social concubines. My complaints were brushed off. The guardian angels made for great school spirit. Only a dozen girls could be cheerleaders, but scores of girls could be guardian angels, scores of girls could inspire the boys to feats of heroism and athletic prowess on Friday nights.

The football team had a perfect record that season.

I couldn't help feeling smug, for they lost every game.

A month into the semester I was also reminded how I wasn't always keen on parental involvement. All teachers had an intervention period in their schedule. It was not an additional planning period. It was a time when teachers were to seek out students who needed academic help. I relished the period. Often I was able to hunt students down in study hall or make an accommodation with another subject matter teacher to work with the student one-to-one during their class. Sometimes I planned and graded during the intervention period, but had students come to my classroom after school. Sometimes I opened the room by 7 A.M. and worked with students who preferred to come in

early. The intervention kept me busy and thinking of ways to be flexible with time.

One morning Mark and Jenny arrived a little after 7:00 A.M. I set
them working together to learn the vocabulary words for our unit on
animation in Film Communication. My third appointment arrived at
7:15. At least I thought it was my third appointment. I barely recognized Missy. Her face was twisted and pained, distorted from tears and
embarrassment. She entered the room, pressed herself against the wall,
and didn't say a word.

A man followed fast behind her and strode toward my desk. He was
short, wore a ball cap, and, like me, had a full beard.

"She tells me you asked her to come in for special help this morning." His tone was a whiplash, skeptical, cynical, insinuating.

Mark and Jenny glanced up from their study.

Missy's face contorted further. Some sophomores in my first period
class hovered near the door, listening.

"Two boys were hanging around the house last night," he sneered.

"That's right," I said. "I asked Missy to come at 7:15 so I could help
her with some school work."

Missy stood rigidly against the wall, the skin around her eyes fes-
tered red.

"So," the man said, turning around to face Missy, and beginning to
walk toward the door, "for once in your life you didn't lie."

In a moment he was gone. Missy didn't move. I waited some seconds for Father Knows Best to make his way down the hall.

"Would you like to go to the restroom, Missy?"

She hesitated, then nodded, and fled the room.

When she returned in a few minutes, I was talking to Jenny and
Mark. Missy took her usual seat and got out her film communication
book. I walked over and sat opposite her. I tried to act like nothing had
happened, that the sophomores weren't lingering by the door, that
Mark and Jenny hadn't witnessed everything. I explained to Missy the
concepts she had confused on the test. I was self-conscious, could hear
myself yammering. Missy stared desperately at the book, avoided my
eyes, held herself together.

The last period of the day, Missy came to film class and took her
seat. She opened her book and gazed at it intently. I didn't know what

had passed between father and daughter. I didn't know the back-story or context. Still, the scene that morning had been ugly. When her father learned that Missy had been telling him the truth, he'd met that information with disdain and sarcasm. What would he have done if he'd caught her in a lie?

Despite the sexist atmosphere that pervaded the school and the unsettling scene with Missy's father, my teaching—my actual classroom work with teenagers—was as fulfilling as it had ever been. Maybe more so, since I was running on the renewed vigor that graduate school had provided. My work with the third graders the previous year made me pay more attention to the growth and development of my students. I had to look harder, though. Children were more open and readable than teenagers. Teenagers cloaked.

The students lurking about the classroom door the morning Missy's miscreant father showed up were part of a doozy of a group to initiate me back to high school teaching. Twenty-three sophomores, only two of them girls (and one of the girls—an unabashed kid who added instant energy and spirit to the class—moved out of the district within a week. Not a good omen.). That left the boys, who were mostly Skoal dippin', Hank Williams Jr. listenin', "I ain't writing or at least I ain't writing much" lovable ne'er-do-wells. There was one football player in the group: Scott, a robust young man with sinewy forearms and thick fingers. He was gentle as a pup and quick with a smile. I don't remember if he was gangsta or a Ramboite—probably both.

I rolled up my metaphorical sleeves, determined to put my egalitarian ideas about teaching writing to the test. I'd get these boys—and the one girl, god bless her—to write. I wrote with them. I demonstrated my writing process, nudging them in conferences to identify their territories and to write about what they knew. That turned out to be, among other topics, motorcycles, bicycle races, the haunted house in town, pit bulls, cider making, and castrating pigs. I was back in the real world of semi-rural, southwestern Ohio.

The boys were one class I couldn't kiss off. I was prepared every day. We had work to do. Those boys had to see my commitment to literacy every class period. They had to know that I read their words and took them seriously. They had to know I respected their subject matter ("Balls to the Walls," as the pig castration narrative came to be called, was published in *Menagerie* that spring). Most of the boys were used to physical exertion in which they sweated and accomplished something tangible, like negotiating a dirt bike course or driving a tractor and tilling a field. We wrote and wrote. In other craft disciplines, students painted, sculpted, sketched plans, sawed wood, glued joints, cut patterns, and sewed garments. In writing class we wrote.

In the beginning, most of them couldn't go five minutes without their fingers cramping. That became a nonissue the more we wrote. They read books they wanted to read, on topics that interested them. They kept journals. Every few weeks they brought a piece of writing entirely through a writing process from a blank page to reading aloud their piece in front of the class while sitting on a stool the shop teacher had given to me. Instead of the "authors chair," as Don Graves and Jane Hansen had called it (1983), we named it "the author's stool," which worked at the time but made me later laugh at the unintended double entendre. But now that I think of it, the Writer's Stool was in keeping with the boys' scatological humor.

That first period class kept me on my teacherly toes.

In another course, Dawn, a senior, read *The Grapes of Wrath* for independent reading. She completely immersed herself in the saga of Tom Joad, his family, and thousands of Okies who made their way to the promised land of California to find prejudice, low wages, hunger, and injustice. Dawn didn't just eat *Grapes*. She gobbled it up. For awhile Steinbeck's 1930s became more vivid to her than contemporary southwestern Ohio.

I brought in my copy of Steinbeck's *A Life in Letters* for her. Dawn carried that thick book around for a week, reading what Steinbeck had written to friends and editors about his Pulitzer-Prize–winning novel and the Great Depression.

One weekend she rented John Ford's 1940, black-and-white adaptation of the novel, starring Henry Fonda. Dawn and her dad watched it twice. At one point, Dawn told me, her dad leapt from the couch, pointed to the screen, and shouted, "Ronald Reagan needs to watch this!"

In another class, students were slogging through Hawthorne's *The Scarlet Letter*. They struggled gamely with the elevated vocabulary, the complex sentence structure, the plentiful narrative summary, and the dearth of dialog. One afternoon, Melody ventured an observation: "I don't see how Reverend Dimmesdale had it in him to produce a passionate moment to create Pearl."

"Oh, I understand," Sharon said. "My parents are just like that, and they have four kids."

Later in the year, in the spring, with me pushing poetry now, both the reading of it and the writing of it, one boy said to me, "Mr. Romano, I gotta say, I don't like poetry. It's too much like the opera instead of the ball game."

"Dwayne," I said, "for these next two weeks, in the poems you write, I want you to go to the ball game." And he did.

Another student, Carmon, wrote lovingly about her history as a writer. Her second-grade teacher had typed one of her poems and published it in a book. "I learned to hold a poem," Carmon said.

I was struck by the importance of holding a poem—holding it in your hands, in your mind, in your heart. It was about this time I began to read a modern free-verse poem at the beginning of every class period, a poem I thought would be accessible in one reading. To make sure I gave the poem the best oral interpretation I could, I practiced saying the words aloud, experimenting with inflection, pace, and meaning. I knew that poetry lay hidden in students. It once had lived vitally in them, when they were children and described fountains as "jumping water," flower petals as "eye lashes," and weeping willows as "drifty looking."

It was good to be back teaching high school students, especially teaching them how to write, accompanying them on their journey toward deeper, wider literacy, being a companion for their words.

I was glad I had gone to the University of New Hampshire. I'd thought I was going to stay longer. I'd thought I was going to get a doctorate. The first few weeks back at Edgewood, however, confirmed to me that quitting graduate school was the right decision. I felt safe and useful, competent and strong. I knew I was where I belonged.

31

clearing the way

"You were quite disciplined," said my friend and former student teacher, John Gaughan. He was talking about my dedication to writing my first book during that reentry year to high school teaching. I was unswerving, afraid that if I didn't begin furiously digging that ditch I'd never complete it. I'd drafted five chapters over the summer. Three I sent to Heinemann. Two I wrote in August while Heinemann made up its mind whether to award me a contract.

I needed large chunks of time to organize material and conceptualize the possible movement of a chapter I'd planned. That meant weekends. I rose at 6:30 A.M., treating myself to an extra half-hour of sleep than I got through the week. I kept those mornings sacrosanct, a vocabulary word I taught my students. Weekend afternoons I often had to attend to teaching matters—grading papers, planning, organizing, reading and rereading literature. Monday holidays meant I could work for a three-day stretch. Thanksgiving break was writerly bliss—five consecutive days of writing. And the Christmas break? Well, that was manna each morning and honey each afternoon.

I wasn't much good drafting anything new through the week. No time and not much mental alertness left after teaching throughout the day and spending another two or three hours reading student work or creating lessons. I could, however, work on a manuscript that was underway. My habit was to print on Sunday evening my weekend's writing. During the next week, then, whenever I had an hour or two, whether at school or at home, I reread the printed copy, tinkering and revising. Working with my own words on paper stimulated my thinking.

I'd pull out a draft, take a favorite pen, and begin to reread. Soon I thought of more to say and wrote between the lines and in the margins. Sometimes I'd write extended passages on a legal pad and staple that page to the manuscript. I'd find words, phrases, sentences, paragraphs that weren't pulling their weight or had wandered off topic. With a certain giddiness, I struck them out. This kind of linguistic weeding was far more pleasurable than weeding the garden. Sometimes I was content just noting a troublesome spot that would require more data gathering, more research, more rethinking and drafting. That was work for Saturday and Sunday. Through the week I could also do grunt work—typing in revisions, printing new copy, creating order from my notes.

I still had companions for my words. Friends John and Mark and colleagues Carolyn and Phyllis at Edgewood read my drafts. Talking over the ideas made me eager to write more. I sent Philippa Stratton two chapters a month, as we had agreed. She kept a steady stream of typed letters coming my way. Sometimes she merely acknowledged receiving the mailing and said she looked forward to reading the chapters. Other times she wrote me detailed responses. I was not alone in the writing.

So much that happened that year worked its way into the book. I continued to lead workshops about teaching writing for the Ohio Writing Project. Whenever I could, I tied the book to the workshops, finding or creating writing and materials I could use for both. Current students and classroom experiences also became subject matter. The chapter on evaluation—the topic I didn't want to go near because of my idiosyncratic ways—came right out of that class of recalcitrant sophomore boys.

My reading that year influenced my teaching, and then both the reading and the teaching influenced my writing. I read a description in the Boynton/Cook catalog of *An Alternate Style: Options in Composition* (1980) by Winston Weathers. The subject piqued my interest. Weathers made a compelling case for writing powerfully by breaking standard rules of writing. I asked Max Morenberg if he thought the book would appeal to me.

"For your own writing it might," said Max. "It won't help you teach writing."

He was right; he was wrong. *An Alternate Style* profoundly influenced both my writing and my teaching. Weathers showed examples of many of our revered writers breaking standard rules of punctuation, spelling, usage, and norms of voice and narrative, all in an effort to write well. He mounted a driving argument in support of the thesis that student writers—and he was writing about college students—should be made aware of *all* the rhetorical options available to them *as* they learned to write. None of this learning the rules first, and then learning to break them.

Weathers supported his thesis by showing the writing of professionals and students who had achieved effective writing by using, among other rhetorical strategies, sentence fragments, lists, labyrinthine sentences, double voices, and orthographic variations. He showed how students could create essays with a series of crots—short, vivid pieces of writing that were like color slides, each making an individual point, but more importantly, having a cumulative effect, a gestalt, like a slide show. Together the crots could emotionally, as well as intellectually, affect readers.

Weathers' alternate style went right into my junior-senior writing class. I created a handout of explanations and examples of various kinds of rule breaking. I got my students experimenting and led them to write alternate-style essays. Their work was exhilarating, like nothing I'd seen before. So imbued was I with Weathers' alternate-style techniques that I wrote one chapter of *Clearing the Way* under its influence: "Literary Warnings," the chapter in which Don Murray said I beat up on university literature teachers. (I guess I'm guilty there. "Touché!" I say. Some lit professors had beat up on me.)

How dedicated, crazed, and obsessive was I that year writing *Clearing the Way*? Here's how much: One Saturday morning when Mariana had taken off for ice skating practice, I sat in front of my computer closing in on finishing a chapter. Kathy appeared in my office doorway. I pulled my attention from the computer screen, impatient to see what she wanted. She wore her winter coat and was barefoot and bare legged. She opened the coat.

"Just a couple more paragraphs," I gulped.

Once the school year ended, I continued to work on the book through June and July. On July 28th, I wrapped the three hundred double-spaced pages in string, placed them in a box, and sent it by UPS to

Heinemann for $3.35. No fanfare. No trumpets. Just a lot of loud music
and television chatter by late morning generated by relatives who were
visiting.

I knew that further work on the book would be required. Philippa
would send the manuscript to two readers. They would write critiques.
I'd talk them over with Philippa, then spend more weeks revising and
adjusting the manuscript. There would be copyediting to review. There
would be page proofs to check. I had agreed to create an Index myself. *Clearing the Way* wasn't scheduled for publication until spring.
Even with all that ahead, I still thought that on the day I sent the manuscript to Heinemann, there would be more. I'd done a big thing, something I hadn't been sure I could do. I'd produced 74,000 final draft
words. Don Murray was right—the joy of writing was in the doing, not
the done. If you depended on accolades for fulfillment, you weren't
much of a writer. Still, I felt melancholy that morning. Sending the
manuscript to Heinemann seemed anticlimactic.

A month later, I received a telephone call.

"Is this Tom Romano, the author?"

"Well," I said. "I've been working on some things."

"Is this Tom Romano who has just written a book? This is Don Murray calling from Nova Scotia."

"Don!" I said.

"I've just finished reading your book. I don't know whether I'm supposed to tell you this, but I'm one of your readers."

"Philippa hadn't said."

"I just blew it then," Don said. "Minnie Mae and I are on vacation.
I brought thirty manuscripts with me. You've written an extraordinary
book, Tom. There's nothing out there like it."

"I was trying to do that."

"You succeeded," Don said. "I'll be writing you a more detailed response. There are things you have to spell out so teachers can know
exactly what to do."

More to spell out? Gladly. I was floating. Don Murray thought I'd
written a fine book. The writing is what mattered, but the accolades
weren't bad.

In the next several months, I completed the remaining work on the
book. The other reader of the manuscript was Linda Rief, a new friend

from New Hampshire and a stellar language arts teacher at Oyster River Middle School in Durham. (Before I learned it was she who had written the second critique, when I groused to Kathy about the reviewer comments, I referred to Linda as "that woman.") Don had wanted me to be more explicit in my council to teachers. He thought I could add lists of clear, specific strategies that teachers could try. Linda liked the vivid scenes I'd rendered of my classroom and students. She wanted to see more of that. She pointed out places where I had lapsed into telling when I should have been showing. For three days I mulled over their praise, criticism, and desires, then got to work.

Revisiting the manuscript after six weeks was like reuniting with a friend. You knew each other well, but had forgotten particulars. As I reread, I was hit with one surprise after another—of ideas, of student writing, of persuasive lines of argument, of turns of language. That was heartening. I also saw places where I could add some of what Murray wanted, some of what Linda wanted, and some new scenes and language that I suddenly wanted.

The book was on schedule for publication. *Clearing the Way*, my book about teaching writing to high school students, and *In the Middle*, Nancie Atwell's remarkable book about teaching reading and writing to middle school students, appeared the same month: March 1987.

32

publication

~

*[P]ublication is not all that it is cracked up to be. But writing is.
Writing has so much to give, so much to teach, so many surprises.
That thing you had to force yourself to do—the actual act of writing—
turns out to be the best part. It's like discovering that while you thought
you needed the tea ceremony for the caffeine, what you really needed
was the tea ceremony. The act of writing turns out to be its own
reward.*

—ANNE LAMOTT, *Bird by Bird*

In January 1987, I attended a three-day seminar at the Poynter Institute for Media Studies in St. Petersburg, Florida. The Poynter folks and Don Murray invited a group of two dozen people to participate. Half were prominent journalists, half were prominent teachers of writing. The teachers were Don Murray, Don Graves, Shirley Brice Heath, Janet Emig, Peter Elbow, Toby Fulwiler, Nancie Atwell, Eliot Wiggenton, and Janie Guilbault. I'd weaseled my way in because of Murray, I'm sure. There was a broad array of top-flight journalists, too: syndicated columnists, feature writers, and editors. The Poynter folks had keen interest in both quality writing and the mentoring of young journalists. The teachers, they thought, could learn something about writing from the journalists. The journalists, in turn, could learn something about teaching from the teachers.

It didn't work out that way. The teachers and journalists were like oil and water. Nothing on a grand scale came out of the seminar. No influential publication. No video series. No new course of study. The camaraderie was great, though, although the journalists pretty much hung with journalists and the teachers pretty much hung with teachers. I met some interesting folks in both camps. Poynter made small grants available for collaboration and projects. I used a grant to cover my expenses when I drove from Durham, New Hampshire, to Fitchburg, Massachusetts, to interview young adult novelist, Robert Cormier (Romano 1990).

On the last day of the seminar, as we were taking leave, some of us lingering around the seminar table, Janet Emig said to me, "Some very good things are going to happen to you with the publication of your book."

"I shouldn't be apprehensive?" I asked her.

"Not at all. Just enjoy it."

I got home from school late one Thursday afternoon—March 19, 1987. Sitting on the desk chair in my office was a package from Purolater Courier. It was open. Inside were ten copies of *Clearing the Way*. I took one copy into the family room and sat on the couch. I was surprised by how emotional I felt. The book looked wonderful; it was meant to grab readers' attention. The cover was glossy with a black background, the title in big red letters in the top quarter. The subtitle under it was yellow: *Working with Teenage Writers*. My name appeared in red lettering just below a photo of two good-looking teenagers— a girl and a boy—who were talking about a piece of writing. They didn't look anything like my Skoal dippin' sophomores from two years earlier. In the background, pieces of writing hung from a bulletin board. I found out later that the setting where Jim Whitney had shot the photo was Linda Rief's eighth grade classroom at Oyster River Middle School. The students weren't Linda's. They were two freshmen from UNH. Junior high and college—that seemed a suitable frame for my high school students.

Mariana, sixteen then and preparing for her driver's test, arrived in the living room with much commotion. I looked up, still holding the book, my thumb against the edge of the pages, touching their bulk. I suppose I looked ready to burst into tears.

"Yeah," Mariana said, "I forgot. Your book arrived. Let's go driving."

That evening I took a copy to Mary Fuller, co-director of the Ohio Writing Project. I wanted to share the book with someone who cared beside family. Mary and I had been friends since I'd met her at the Writing Project six years earlier. She had just put baby Juliana to bed. The apartment was quiet and dimly lit. Mary made tea. We sat at the dining room table. She happily paged through the book, dipping in to read here and there, generally making me feel pretty good as she engaged in a think-aloud of what she was experiencing.

The next day I took copies to Edgewood. On the table in the empty teachers' lounge lay Phyllis' satchel and cup of coffee. I heard the copier phtting away in the workroom down the hallway. I laid a copy of *Clearing the Way* by Phyllis' coffee cup, then left the room. When I returned, she was reading. She rose and hugged me.

Later in my classroom, I placed the books on my desk. All day kids handled them and passed them around. Rebecca, one of my students, had taken candid black-and-white photos of me in the fall as I circulated through the room engaging in writing conferences. Heinemann had used one of the photos on the back cover beside my bio. Rebecca beamed about her photo credit.

Norma, a senior whom I'd taught the previous year, popped her head around the doorway. "Hey!" she said, waltzing up an aisle. "What's this I hear about a book?"

I extended a copy to her. She held it in both hands. "This is hot!" she said, pumping it up and down. "This is hot!"

∿∿∿

After third period, I came upstairs to the office to check my mail and go to lunch. On the office counter was a monstrosity of an artificial flower arrangement, purple, feathery, and gaudy. My mind flashed to that satiric Frank Oz film, *Little Shop of Horrors*, about a plant that feeds on human blood. I passed the counter fast, retrieved my mail, and headed for the door.

"Mr. Romano," called a secretary, "that flower arrangement's for you. You'll want to take it to your room."

I went back to the counter and opened the note. It was from my mom: "Congratulations, Tommy!"

I suddenly knew where all that purple would look great.

∿∿∿

My mother lived four hours away in Canton, Ohio. When she learned the book was published, before I could even mail her a copy, she went to Waldenbooks, where she often bought paperbacks. ("A good mystery with a little sex," she once told me. "That's what I want in my books.")

She asked the clerk if they had that new book by Tom Romano, *Clearing the Way*.

He didn't think so, he said. He hadn't heard of it, but he would check.

"It's just out," said my mother.

"No," he said. "I don't see it listed."

Mom was incredulous, a little miffed, in fact, since she was such a good customer. She couldn't understand how a major bookstore chain could not have this important new book on its shelves.

"You're missing sales," she said to the clerk. "I know the author. He's a magnificent writer!"

The clerk promised to order copies.

My sister, Nancy, lived in Malvern, Ohio, where we had both grown up, where our father had operated the bar and bowling alleys for so many years. She contacted Heinemann and ordered a copy of *Clearing the Way*. When the book arrived, she took it straight to the high school library and made sure it was put on the shelf.

Our friend, Cathy Gaughan, sent the local weekly newspaper a photo of me and two paragraphs that her husband, my good friend, John, had written to announce publication of the book. Three weeks passed and nothing appeared in the newspaper. "What's going on?" Mariana asked me. "Doesn't the paper consider you a prominent enough citizen?"

Don Murray called. He was at a conference in Atlanta.

"Guess what I'm sitting here caressing?" he said. Philippa had given him a copy of *Clearing the Way*.

"When I read the dedication to your mother," Don said, "I got tears in my eyes." I'd actually dedicated the book to three women: my daughter, my wife, and my mother. (I couldn't imagine writing another book. I had to make sure I got the dedication right.) Of Mom, I had written:

> My mother, Mae, who won an essay contest in 1930 when she was fifteen. She had written about pottery making, a subject her family knew well. When asked to read her essay, she did and grew increasingly pale and terrified as she stood before her class-mates on that, the last day she ever attended school.

"I read the 'Acknowledgments' too," Don said. "You said nice things about Minnie Mae and nice things about your wife. That's good."

Janet Emig had been right. Good things were happening, and I was enjoying them, even smiling a little at the zeal of my mother and sister. I didn't intend to write a second book. I had used up all my subject matter. I felt barren as the garden in November. I couldn't imagine summoning the concentration of thought, the discipline of focus, and the intensity of labor necessary to write another book.

Don Graves had told me not to feel bad if the book didn't sell very well initially. "It took two years for my first book to take off."

I wouldn't say that sales of *Clearing the Way* ever "took off." But two years later it was selling better than it had in year one. Twenty-one years later it's still in print.

After publication, I started to get calls from school districts to work with teachers about teaching writing. I started to get invited to conferences to give keynote speeches and presentations. In 1988, the English Language Arts Council of the Alberta Teachers' Association held its spring conference at Chateau Lake Louise in the Rocky Mountains. The theme of the conference was Clearing the Way. I was asked to keynote. They'd even had bookplate stickers made with the title.

I began this chapter with a quotation from Anne Lamott's *Bird by Bird*. My experience with the publication of *Clearing the Way* makes me want to argue with her. I can't though. Publishing is sweet, but writing is sweeter. I'm never more fulfilled than when I have a writing project and time to do it. During the previous school year, amid working a full-time job, between fathering and husbanding, I hadn't *found* time to write. I'd *made* time to write. Some things suffered. I didn't cook as much. I missed some of my daughter's swim meets. I holed up more and spent less time with friends and family. I was preoccupied sometimes when I should have been focusing all my attention on something else.

Still, it was great to dig this ditch, this ditch that I wanted to dig, but wasn't sure I could, this ditch that others had encouraged me to dig. It was good to travel the path toward publication. It was good to create, to experience the surprises that attended language, to encounter mental and emotional obstacles and overcome them, to keep on when I might have quit, to prevail over something I had control of. I didn't zig. I didn't zag.

It was great, too, to have dug the ditch, to stand by it, relaxed, relieved, proud. It was great to have a clap on the back from people I respected.

"What are you going to write next?" Don Murray asked me.

33

the way I'd like
to teach

played shortstop on a stellar little league baseball team when I was
twelve. We won every game during the regular season—twenty.
Greg Alexander caught and pitched occasionally. Charlie pitched
and played outfield (eight years later he was an offensive guard for Ohio
State). My cousin, David, played first base. Jackie played third. Teddy
pitched and caught.

Late in the season we nearly lost a game to Magnolia, a team we'd
beaten twice in May. I learned later that our manager, Mr. Dunn,
thought a loss might have been good for us. The tournament was coming up, and he believed we'd gotten cocky.

Charlie pitched, and the Magnolia batters beat up on him so badly
that his father sitting in the stands was furious. His face was purple. He
screamed at Mr. Dunn to take Charlie out. Mr. Dunn left him in. By
the time Charlie pitched out of trouble, we were down seven to
nothing.

We started coming back. We weren't undefeated for nothing. That
entire season I hit two home runs, but wouldn't you know, I hit one
that game. I was as surprised as anyone when the ball lifted over the
right field fence. Our rally was on.

Charlie hit a home run, too. He was furious, just like his dad, angry,
frustrated, and embarrassed. He tore around the bases like a lunatic,
the Magnolia infielders hopping out of his way.

In the top of the last inning we were down one run, 7 to 6. I reached
third base with two outs, my friend Jackie at bat. "Play it safe," our third
base coach said to me. "Stay close to the bag and *don't* get picked off."

Jackie wasn't a home-run hitter, but he was reliable. Magnolia's catcher, a boy I'd been playing ball against for several years, had been dropping pitches the entire game. That's how I'd gotten to third.

Jackie was down to his last strike. He looked about ready to cry with all the pressure on him to save our undefeated season. The next pitch, a ball, bounced off the catcher's glove and squirted to his right. I broke for home. The catcher flipped off his mask, scrambled after the ball. I slid but it wasn't even close. Tie game.

I wasn't fast, but I understood the game and was smart running the bases. My steal of home was a "heads-up play," as Mr. Dunn always called out when we used brains as well as physical skill.

Jackie took the next pitch for a called third strike.

We held Magnolia scoreless in their half of the sixth. Next inning we beat them 12 to 8. I don't remember celebrating. I was relieved. We'd been lucky. I knew their catcher felt awful.

That summer evening contained my best moment as an athlete. Not because of the home run. That had been surprising and thrilling, but lucky. What I am proud of was that bold move of stealing home. After the game, the third base coach clapped me on the back and said, "Did you hear me send you?" I shook my head. "That's because I didn't."

I knew I'd made the right decision, though, even if Jackie had gotten a hit, even if I had been tagged out. I was *in* the game. At twelve years old in a little league baseball game, I had entered a state of flow, a zone of optimal psychological experience, as one researcher termed it (Csikszentmihalyi 1990). I had the skills necessary to succeed. The situation was challenging. I knew what had to be done—we don't score a run, the game ends, we lose. I was so absorbed by what was happening that time stood still. When the ball skittered to the catcher's right, the last opportunity was there. I acted. It wasn't thinking so much as knowing, instantaneously, intellect and body one.

That's precisely the way I hope to teach. Prepared through study and practice. Alert. Involved. Paying attention. Accurately reading what's happening to my students. Quick to seize teachable moments. Seeing, sensing, learning, and every now and then, taking a risk.

34

of Whitman
and friend

Walt Whitman deserved something dramatic. My high school students and I were reading nineteenth-century American literature. We'd spent a month with The Fireside Poets, those popular poets of American legend and home life, among them Oliver Wendell Holmes, John Greenleaf Whittier, and Henry Wadsworth Longfellow. Their poems were conventionally rhymed and strictly metered. We read of *Old Ironsides* and being snowbound in nineteenth-century New England. We looked afar to see if there was one lantern or two in the belfry of the North Church tower so we could gallop through every Middlesex village and farm on a midnight ride to alert the populace that the British were coming. I had great fun rediscovering The Fireside Poets. They were out of fashion in academia, so I hadn't read them since high school.

My bias, however, was to Whitman. I admired his bold experimentation with free verse at a time in American letters when newspapers, magazines, and book publishers accepted only conventional forms of poetry. I had deepened my knowledge of "the Good Grey Poet" by reading Justin Kaplan's *Walt Whitman: A Life*, the first modern biography I'd ever read. I was delighted to see Kaplan blend scholarship with imagination. He brought to life mid-nineteenth-century New York City with its teeming masses, cultural diversity, and propellent growth. Occasionally, Kaplan used dramatic narrative to bring Whitman to life on the page.

Yes, with these teenagers who'd never heard of him, Whitman deserved something dramatic. I was indebted to Whitman. During my sophomore year at Miami his writing had provided direction when I was wandering, faith when I was faithless, hope when my thoughts of life had become grim.

Yes, Walt Whitman—so crucial to my intellectual, spiritual, and pedagogical development—deserved something dramatic with my students. Moving from The Fireside Poets to Walt Whitman was a monumental leap, one akin to Captain Samuel Brady's mythic twenty-two-foot leap across Ohio's Cuyahoga River to escape pursuing Indians in 1780. I wanted to make my pedagogical leap dramatic in its own right.

The Fireside Poets had been educated, formal, and three-named. Though some were progressive in their political beliefs, their poetry was conventionally written within long-established traditions. In their midst, along came Whitman—not three names, but two, not Walter but Walt. He wrote in expansive, groundbreaking ways, extending boundaries, questioning poetic forms, subject matter, and ideas.

The day we wrapped up The Fireside Poets and began Walt Whitman, I planned a metamorphosis. I dressed in a suit coat, buttoned vest, and properly knotted tie. Although I wore a strategic pair of dungarees, I was still all about formality, protocol, and delicacy in speech, dress, and manner. I said some last words about The Fireside Poets, then, with some ostentation, removed my coat and vest. I pulled off my tie, unfastened the top buttons of the pullover white gauze shirt that had been nicely obscured under vest and coat. I pulled up my pant legs to reveal boots and tucked the ends into them. Lastly, I withdrew a broad-brimmed leather hat from the closet and placed it atop my head.

I was no longer a Fireside Poet. Now I was one of the roughs that Whitman so admired, looking a little like that drawing of Walt that appeared in the first edition of *Leaves of Grass*: Walt with one hand in a pant pocket, the other on a hip, shirt open at the throat, visage benign and confident, gazing directly at the reader. Whitman in 1855 and I at that moment, were close in age. I had a Whitman beard. With the hat on, my bald head did not pull my look away from Walt Whitman, a Kosmos, of Manhattan the son. I sauntered to the head of the class and turned to the students, striking an insouciant pose. From memory I spoke Whitman's words

> I celebrate myself, and sing myself,
> And what I assume you shall assume,
> For every atom belonging to me as good belongs to you.

I moved about the classroom, using my voice to communicate Whitman's wonder, to create an atmosphere, to invite students in.

> I loafe and invite my soul,
> I lean and loafe at my ease observing a spear of summer
>   grass.
>
> My tongue, every atom of my blood, form'd from this soil,
>   this air,
> Born here of parents born here from parents the same, and
>   their parents the same,
> I, now thirty-seven years old in perfect health begin,
> Hoping to cease not till death.
>
> Creeds and schools in abeyance,
> Retiring back a while sufficed at what they are, but never
>   forgotten,
> I harbor for good or bad, I permit to speak at every hazard,
> Nature without check with original energy. ([1855] 1981, 27)

And thus we were off. We read and talked about Walt Whitman, examining his vision of America, considering and testing his ideas of God and soul and life and death. What did it mean to harbor for good or bad, to speak at every hazard with original energy? What had that meant for Whitman in the nineteenth century? What did it mean for students as they moved toward crafting their own songs of themselves? We found out. We wrote.

35

multigenre

~~~

Mid-May, 1988. Not much school left. Not many more written words by 150 teenagers. It was evening. My daughter, home from track practice, had commandeered the family room. She ate left-over broccoli and cheese casserole, talked on the telephone, kept an eye on a television sitcom, and somewhere amid all that did homework.

One room away I sat at my desk, a glass of red wine within reach, a stack of research papers near. I was undaunted. These papers were the fruition of a new research assignment I'd tried with high school seniors. Instead of producing one long expository paper, students wrote about their topics in many genres. Although each piece was self-contained, making a point of its own, taken together, all the writing created a unified whole. I called the assignment a *multigenre research paper*.

I reached for the first one. Brian's. What a great kid. School plays, musicals, chorus—a delightful young man who combined intellect, wit, and irresistible charm. Students from every clique in school liked Brian. Teachers, too, from the chemistry lab to the art room. Brian had written his multigenre research paper about John Lennon, his musical-social-political hero. Brian was nine years old when Lennon was murdered. He titled his paper, "The Long and Wonderful Odyssey of the Walrus—A Heart Play."

I turned to the first piece of writing:

Unfinished Music #1—John

He hit the pavement
ass-first
Yoko raised
his

head.
He wanted to embrace her
but a hundred people
were
standing on
his arms.
  Oh, God, Yoko, I've been shot (Romano 1995, 122)

I stopped sipping wine. I heard neither the sitcom's laugh track nor my daughter's occasional outbursts of personality. I was rapt, immersed in a world of fact and imagination, surprises of language, information, and creativity—all this woven together by a high school kid. At that point in my career, I had sixteen years' experience. I'd written a book about my work. I consulted with school systems, writing project sites, and university language arts programs. I'd been around. I was no rookie. Still, during these weeks in May when high school seniors showed me what could be done with multigenre, I sensed my teaching of writing, my very career, changing forever.

Two years earlier, in August, after I'd sent Heinemann the *Clearing the Way* manuscript, Kathy, Mariana, and I traveled to Stratford, Ontario, to the Shakespeare Festival—my idea of a vacation for the family. In two days we saw *Hamlet*, *Macbeth*, and *A Man for All Seasons*. Between plays one afternoon we went to Fanfare Books, a magnificent old house of a bookstore. The place was so jammed with books that they were displayed as though in a library.

I moved along the shelves with my head tilted, reading the spines of the books. I blinked at a title I just had to pull from the shelf: *The Collected Works of Billy the Kid* by Michael Ondaatje (1984 [1970]). What was this? Billy the Kid had been an outlaw, a killer, not a writer who collected his works. I opened the book and paged through, reading here and there. What I read looked like poems, deeply rich in imagery, stark, and sometimes sweetly ambiguous. I hadn't heard of the author. What I read, though, I liked, more in my muscles and bones than my head, so I bought this offbeat collection of poetry.

When I got back to Ohio and read Ondaatje's first book, I found it was no collection of poems. Just over a hundred pages, the text's subject matter was roughly the last three years of the life of William H. Bonney, alias Billy the Kid, when he was involved in the bloody Lincoln County War in New Mexico, the John Tunstall-Alexander McSween faction versus the Lawrence Murphy-James Dolan-John Riley faction for economic supremacy in the county—English versus Irish in 1878 New Mexico.

Ondaatje's book was like no other I'd read. Not strictly poetry, though there were many poems. Not a novel, though it contained dramatic narratives. Not a biography, though it contained biographically accurate facts about Billy and the people involved in his life. The book told a story through poems, songs, a newspaper interview, dramatic narratives, photographs, a genuine comic book legend, posters, and extended quotations from other published books. Many points of view were represented. Ondaatje stayed out of the story he was weaving, mainly, though on the final page there is a photo of him as a child in cowboy regalia, toy six-guns in each hand. The book was demanding to read, leaving it to the reader to piece together the genres.

Here is what most intrigued me about the book: Ondaatje joined fact with imagination. He took actual events and characters and rendered them as dramatic scenes to reveal emotional truth. When truth had been lost to history or was up for debate, Ondaatje created new truth, new possibility. We know, for example, that Sheriff Pat Garrett and his deputies caught up with Billy and his gang hiding out in a one-room cabin in a place called Stinking Springs, New Mexico. We know that Garrett killed one of the gang. We know that Billy and the others surrendered. Ondaatje uses these bones to imagine the situation in vivid detail: snow on boots, bullets in belly, gun barrel poking into the ground, Billy's friend fatally wounded, pissing his pants, warning Billy to watch out for the mess.

In an incredible poem late in the book, Ondaatje writes of Billy dying in the seconds after he is shot by Garrett. Ondaatje imagines himself into Billy's voice: "the bullet itch frozen" in his head, his "brain coming out like red grass," one surreal image after another, repeating in flashes previous images and motifs from early in the book, dramatically capturing "the end of it" (1970, 95).

I didn't understand all of the book. As much as it provided complex characterizations, vivid writing, surprising multiple genres, and a subtle cohesiveness, I was puzzled by much of it. What was the meaning of the repulsive story of Livingstone and his dogs? Who was Angela D? Still, I wondered, could my students do this? Could they research someone of their choice and instead of writing a traditional research paper—a single-voiced monolog—could they create a blend of genres, voices, and points of view? Could they learn facts about their topic and combine those facts with imagination to render intellectual and emotional truths?

I believed they could.

Could I risk five weeks one semester and lead students into multigenre, a territory I myself had not explored?

I believed I could.

I broke for home.

The next spring I piloted a multigenre project with a group of high school seniors. There were some excellent writers in the class—Brian, for example. There were also students who'd taken courses with me as sophomores or juniors and wanted another. There was even a student who needed one more English credit and thought that this class smacked of "creative" and might be an easy go of it. (After all, a guidance counselor had told him, how can you grade creativity?)

I've taught multigenre every year but two since 1988, and those two years I did not teach. Professionally, I suppose I am most identified with multigenre. I've taught classes about multigenre at Miami University, the University of New Hampshire, and on Martha's Vineyard. I've taught multigenre to high school students, undergraduates, and graduate students. I've gotten better and better at it.

I've written a lot about multigenre. Articles and one book: *Blending Genre, Altering Style: Writing Multigenre Papers* (2000). In a video series produced by Kentucky Educational Television, I've touted the teaching of multigenre to middle school students. Graduate students have developed a website for me: www.users.muohio.edu/romanots/. On it you'll find an annotated bibliography of publications about multigenre. You'll find assignments, research designs, rubrics, and multigenre papers by my students at Miami.

Two other teachers have written fine books about teaching students to write multigenre papers: Camille Allen's *The Multigenre Research Paper: Voice, Passion, and Discovery in Grades 4–6* (2001), and Melinda

Putz's *A Teacher's Guide to the Multigenre Research Paper: Everything You Need to Get Started* (2006). I use ideas from their books in my own teaching.

Here is my straight definition of multigenre:

> A multigenre paper arises from research, experience, and imagination. It is not an uninterrupted, expository monolog, nor a seamless narrative, nor a collection of poems. A multigenre paper is composed of many genres and subgenres. Each piece works by itself, is self-contained, makes a point of its own. Yet all the pieces are connected by theme or topic and sometimes by language, images, and content. In addition to many genres, a multigenre paper often contains many voices, not just the author's. The craft demanded of the writer is to make such a paper hang together as one.

I like that expository definition. It's direct, clear, and simple. Exposition is a useful mode of writing, often just right for explaining and analyzing. I also like the following definition that I wrote in the spirit of multigenre:

> I am what I am. I am imagination, metaphor, images that make you see and wonder and speculate. I am the enigmatic final line of a poem you carry for days. I am what I am. I resist exposition, though I am not averse to it. I am opposition to a strict writing diet of thesis-driven, argumentative essays. I am what I am. I am the lash in the eye of tradition. I am not thesis, though I am pointed. I am "so what" to those who demand that everything be explained. I am a force against the prosaic, and that does not mean writing in prose. I am what I am. I am implicitly emphatic. I am, as Whitman wrote, "Expecting the main things from you." I am what I am. I am the high-wire act without a net. I am not above falling on my face. I am what I am. I am Pandora's Rhetorical Box. I am many and I am one. I am one and I am many. I am not mashed potatoes. I am cioppino. I am trust me, travel along with me, be patient. I am telling you by showing you. I am multigenre.

36

clear decision

"Why don't you come back?" Tom Newkirk said to me. The two of us were standing in his kitchen. That summer of 1988 I'd taught at the Literacy Institute at the University of New Hampshire. Kathy had joined me at the end of it for some vacation time. Mariana had come along and was attending field hockey camp at the university. Tom and Beth Newkirk had invited Kathy and me to a lobster dinner that evening. I hadn't had Tom for a class four years earlier that year I was in graduate school, but I knew him as an integral part of the Ph.D. program.

"You're a leader in the profession," he said. "You've got a book, so we know you can write a dissertation. You've just got to get additional coursework."

I listened intently. Tom Newkirk was a persuasive man, a first-rate intellect, a teacher whose opinions are informed, humane, and grounded in reality.

His question took me by surprise. My teaching at Edgewood and my work with teachers was going so well that I'd never considered for a moment going back to graduate school. Don Murray, in fact, had told me I'd made the right decision. "Writing the book," he said, "will be much more important in the long run." After that evening at Tom and Beth's, though, I thought plenty about graduate school.

I talked over the possibility with Kathy. Returning to UNH to finish the doctoral program was tempting, despite the way I'd crashed and burned earlier. Yet just then, I was professionally fulfilled in so many ways: teaching adolescents, working with colleagues I cared for and respected, writing a book, developing new curriculum, working with teachers from my strength in the classroom.

In August before Edgewood resumed, I went to the Canadian Conference of Teachers of English in St. Johns, Newfoundland, another invitation that had come as a result of *Clearing the Way*. I presented the work my students had recently done with alternate style and multigenre. One presenter at the conference was Lorri Neilsen, who had recently received her Ph.D. from UNH. We'd entered the reading and writing doctoral program the same year. She had been part of that stellar Mast Way research team. Participating in the conference, listening to Lorri and others talk about their research, the question Newkirk had put to me—all this had my mind racing. I took time with my journal and jotted the things that excited me about the profession, the things I had real verve for: my teaching, the writing my high school students were doing, working with teachers, writing about my passions. I reached a clear decision.

No.

I did not need a doctorate.

I loved what I was doing. I loved the atmosphere I was doing it in. Life was very good, and I'm not one to use *very* very often.

No, I would not return to the University of New Hampshire in any capacity but as a teacher in the summer literacy institute.

37

a good run done

When I was sixteen, the girl I'd been going with for ten months broke up with me. On the afternoon of our break up, she said, with a snarl in her voice, "What did you think? That you'd just keep coming up to see me every Saturday night and everything would be hunky-dory?"

Well . . . yes.

I still had faith that Edgewood would remain a good place to work even though monumental changes had taken place. Roger, that inclusive, visionary superintendent, had moved on to another school district, in large part driven out by the good ol' boy network. Gene Smith, my beloved principal, had applied for the superintendent's position, but didn't get it. He was made Assistant Superintendent, where he had little power at the district level and no power anymore at the high school. The new principal was Bronson Hammer. He was new to the district, a former shop teacher, a nuts and bolts kind of guy.

Mr. Hammer was skeptical of our writing program. He wanted to know what was going on. In the early days of school he visited my sophomore writing workshop. He sat in the back of the room and watched. I gave a minilesson and led students into ten minutes of non-stop writing with pens flying across paper. I wrote with them, as usual. We sought to tap into that linguistic intelligence we all possess to some degree. I wanted students to experience it and learn to put language to work for them.

While we wrote, Mr. Hammer rose from the desk and wandered about the classroom, his hands on his hips, looking at what was posted on the wall. My mistake. I should have prepped him before class, explained what I would be doing and why I was doing it. I should have invited him to write with us and mentioned the implicit message he would send to students if he joined them as a writer. After the writing prompt, the class moved into workshop mode, the students getting out the writing they had under construction, me circulating about the classroom, conferencing with students at their desks. Mr. Hammer soon left.

He wanted to meet with Phyllis about the writing program. I joined her. Our writing program made so much sense that we knew if we had the opportunity to explain it to Mr. Hammer that he would understand and value it too. We met in an empty classroom. I brought my notebook, student folders, plans for minilessons. Phyllis explained our philosophy. I chipped in. We showed Mr. Hammer past issues of *Menagerie*. We showed him classroom publications that were copied on the cheap and that every student got something published in. We showed him one student's writing folder.

"What about grammar?" Mr. Hammer wanted to know.

I showed him the three-ring notebook I kept with a page devoted to each of my seventy-five sophomores in writing workshop. It was an idea we had adopted from Atwell's *In the Middle* (1987). On the sheet we noted grammar and usage skills students had mastered and those that were not yet under their control. I explained how students reviewed their personal skill record sheets before editing and polishing their next pieces of writing so they would attend to skills they were weak in.

"That's the best idea I've heard from you yet," said Mr. Hammer. "I went to Catholic school," he said. "The nuns drilled grammar and spelling into us."

Mr. Hammer told us that he was ordering a set of grammar books for each English teacher's classroom.

"No need to do that," Phyllis said, smiling cheerfully. "We already have a good writing handbook we use now and then."

"Not a writing handbook," said Mr. Hammer. "A grammar book."

There had been complaints in the community, he told us, complaints that students weren't learning rules of proper English.

We told him who the complainer was, that she'd been complaining for years.

I told Mr. Hammer that since I had started using writing workshop, following Atwell's classroom management ideas, I paid more attention than ever to students' errors of grammar, usage, punctuation, and spelling, a realization that had surprised me. During editing conferences before they made their final copies, I explicitly taught students the rules they needed.

"I'll expect all English teachers to use the grammar books two or three times a week," said Mr. Hammer. "I want the grammar they're teaching written in lesson plans."

Phyllis said that she'd received a call from Corey Jamison's mother who had thanked her because Corey's writing portfolio had been commended by a writing assessment program at Miami University.

"That's Corey Jamison," said Mr. Hammer. "She'd score well on any writing assessment."

"A big reason Corey's portfolio was so rich," I said, "was because she had written so much. In assembling her portfolio she had a lot of writing to choose from."

"Like I said, Corey's not your typical student."

"You don't think all that writing, conferencing, and revising made her a better writer? That girl developed a writing state of mind, Mr. Hammer."

"I don't know about that," he said. "I just know our students need more grammar and spelling."

"Do you like to write?" Phyllis asked him.

"I hate to write," he said. "My writing is full of mistakes. My wife has to proofread everything."

"I don't understand," I said.

"Don't understand what?" said Mr. Hammer.

"What about all that grammar in Catholic school? Didn't it teach you anything?"

"Aw, I never get that stuff."

The English Department felt embattled. It wasn't just the grammar book. The titular educational leader of the high school—Mr. Hammer—did not value our expertise and experience. He didn't value the students' enthusiasm for writing. Our work with the Ohio Writing Project counted for nothing. Neither did my book. We were convinced that part of Mr. Hammer's behind-closed-doors job description was to weaken the power of the English Department. Our professional talk shifted from conversation about writing, literature, and teaching to the new strictures and to administrators dictating curriculum who knew little about language development and teaching writing.

Every day that fall, I came home complaining. One evening Kathy said, "Why don't you quit? Go back to graduate school."

Two months after my certain, clear decision, I zigged and zagged. The writing program we'd built so carefully over the years was under attack. From a proactive, progressive stance, my colleagues and I were mired in a siege mentality. I wrote Tom Newkirk and asked for reinstatement in the doctoral program.

Teaching at Edgewood was no longer hunky-dory.

6
UNH Reprise

38

Indiana tumble

I returned to UNH in the fall of 1989 and took up residence again in Babcock Hall. The accommodations were perfect for a busy doctoral student, especially one with my slow reading speed and tedious but workable writing process. Housekeeping was minimal. I made my twin bed each morning, a remarkable feat for me that added instant order to my day. I changed sheets every two weeks, washed clothing when needed, swept my room every week of New Hampshire sand that had surreptitiously accumulated.

I ate breakfast and dinner across the road and up the hill amid the trees at Philbrick Dining Hall. Once across the road, there was a stairway of sorts, but I usually took the path covered with pine needles. After pulling on Levis and a sweatshirt, within two minutes I'd be handing my ID to the dining hall lady.

One crisp Saturday morning in September, I finished breakfast, bussed my tray, and headed out. I had a lot of work to do and the entire weekend before me. I pushed through the door into bright sunshine and cool air smelling of pine. I wore a bulky Indiana University sweatshirt, gray with big red lettering. My daughter had sent it to me to mark the start of her freshman year, a good one so far, except for finite math.

Ahead, just emerging from the trees, two undergrads—a guy and a girl—made their way to the dining hall. My left foot set down on the edge of the sidewalk. My ankle turned. I collapsed like a cold-cocked boxer, falling to my left. In some of the quickest thinking I'd ever done, I embraced my momentum and rolled—left side, back, right side, front—and bounced to my feet. The girl's mouth hung open. The boy pumped his fist and shouted, "Good roll!"

It *was* a good roll, perfectly timed and executed. No one was more surprised than I, but there I was on my feet at the University of New Hampshire.

39

digging in

I was careful my second time at UNH. Stayed within my capacities. Pursued my passions within the program. I took two classes instead of three. One class was a reading and writing seminar with Don Graves—a two-semester sequence offered every two years for the doctoral students. There were nine of us, including a young teacher from Maine on sabbatical. We met every Monday morning at Graves' house in the New Hampshire woods outside Durham. Each week I picked up fellow doctoral student, Danling Fu, for the short drive. Danling had been in the United States four years, having already earned a master's degree in English Literature. All this graduate work for her was, of course, in a second language! One morning as we drove through New Hampshire countryside, she said, "You be careful, Tom. You get this degree and end up sounding like Vygotsky!" Yes, good reminder—my voice, my steady center. Maintaining both while I learned and grew was crucial.

My second class was in the English Department with Tom Newkirk, a seminar titled The Cognitive Roots of Composition. We did, in fact, read Vygotsky, and Plato, Montaigne, Rousseau, Dewey, Bruner, Carol Gilligan's *In a Different Voice* (1982), and Newkirk's recent book, *More Than Stories* (1989). For my research paper I dived into collaborative learning, blending theory with my experience teaching high school students.

I had an urgency about my reading that semester. Newkirk told me that I ought to take my written exams in January. I swallowed, but realized he was right. Let's get on with it. This is, after all, the stuff I loved. I got the doctoral reading list, began buying books, and reading and annotating them, taking extensive notes, and typing key passages.

The essence of all this reading I reported on in the one-pagers due each week in Graves' seminar, where there were few assigned texts. We were to read off the reading list and bring learning to the group. I did, with a vengeance.

The first book I read that semester was Mike Rose's masterpiece, *Lives on the Boundary* (1989). The book nailed me. It was a serendipitous connection that was just right for me; a text that offered personal comfort and guidance, a reminder of my journey's beginning. In vigorous, evocative writing Rose combined memoir with description and analysis of his work over the years with underprepared students. He himself had been one of them, the son of immigrants. For a long time Rose had played the part expected of him, rejecting all things academic, essentially, sticking a knife into himself and twisting it purposely.

So moved was I by *Lives on the Boundary* that I got Rose's address from Don Murray and wrote him a letter. I told him of our mutual connections: My father, too, had been an Italian immigrant from near Naples. I, too, had felt anger and disillusionment years earlier in a master's degree program at Miami University, when I ran into literary elitism and intellectual one-upmanship among graduate students in the English department. I told Rose that four years earlier I had quit a Ph.D. program, just as he had once quit a high-powered doctoral program at UCLA. As much as the personal connections meant to me, it was Rose's *academic* writing that struck me most:

> I loved the texture, style, and all inclusiveness of *Lives on the Boundary*. Allusions to Langston Hughes and "Rockin' Robin." The surprising metaphors, like the one you created to sum up the distant scholar who believed that "brutalizing the imagination" was necessary in the campaign to learn skills. . . . That's the way I want to write, Mike, with just such texture and style and all inclusiveness, at least as much as my soul can conjure and as much as the writing will bear.

In just over a week, I received a reply from Rose, that letter speeding to me coast to coast from California to New Hampshire. It was warm and personal, as though we'd known each other for years. The voice in the letter was the voice in the book. He thanked me for the compliments and commented on the parallels between our lives. And then he wrote this that sent me to the dictionary:

> I also want to get avuncular for a minute and encourage you to stick with the PhD this time around. You've got some great folks at UNH; milk them for everything you can and try your best to please but ultimately ignore the rest. This business desperately needs people like you, and once you jump through this hoop, you'll be in a better position to do the things you want to do. I wish you all the best with this; I went through lots of changes, as we used to say, on my way to the PhD, so I know what you're going through.

In addition to an Uncle Tony and an Uncle Gigi, I felt a little like I had an Uncle Mike. And I appreciated it. There was no way I was quitting this time. I also had a compassionate and intellectually rigorous mentor in Tom Newkirk. I'd come to see him as the brightest light in this country in matters of literacy kindergarten through college.

I had a successful first semester. I swam hard but never felt like I was sinking, as I had four years earlier. I didn't lose weight or develop a twitch in my eye. There was no meltdown this time. I had dinner with Don and Minnie Mae Murray every few weeks. I wrote. I read. I did some consulting in teaching writing that came my way. A big deal for me that semester was being asked to give one of the keynote talks at a literacy conference the graduate students sponsored every other year at UNH. The other two speakers were Jane Hansen and Don Graves. I gave the noon talk and spoke about passion and writing.

And then there was a memorable, chance encounter with Newkirk one evening. The methods class I was teaching for my assistantship didn't meet for ten minutes, so I went down to his office. He wasn't in, though the door was open, the light on. I sat down and waited. Tom returned and we chatted. He told me that at the recent conference when he was listening to my keynote, he thought, "What are we trying to do with this guy?" And then he spoke to me directly: "You want to write and work with teachers, don't you?"

"That's exactly what I want to do."

"If you want to be a researcher like Ruth Hubbard, we can teach you to do that, but I don't think that's what you want."

"I want to work with teachers, Tom. I want to teach and write."

That semester ended well. Much hard work and one triumph after another. Much laughter, too, with new friends Danling Fu and Bonnie Sunstein, Peg Voss, and Cathy Yeager. Before Thanksgiving break I attended the NCTE conference in Baltimore, where I conducted a workshop with my friend from Ohio, John Gaughan, and presented with Linda Rief and Georgia Heard about teaching and writing poetry.

Early December was consumed with writing the research paper for Newkirk's seminar. I worked at a card table I set up at the foot of the bed in the dorm room, snow falling outside the narrow window above the heating unit that popped on every twenty minutes to run for five. No matter. I was warmed by work, by the writing in which I told stories, related theory, and connected the two. Once again, I sought to write beyond the class, though my hunch was that Newkirk wanted me to write in a personally public way, something both readable and substantive.

One day in his office, he and I had been talking about collabora-

Top row, left to right: Tom Newkirk *and* Bonnie Sunstein
Bottom row, left to right: Maureen Barbieri *and* Danling Fu

tion. I got up to leave, stood in his doorway. He said, almost offhand-
edly, that even though writing was collaborative in the broadest sense,
we liked to think we wrote alone. We liked to think we had autonomy.
That parting comment made me think of Walt Whitman, of Justin
Kaplan's biography in which he discussed the cultural and intellectual
currents on the move in mid-nineteenth-century America that influenced Whitman's barbaric yawp. I titled my paper, "Writing Through
Others: The Necessity of Collaboration" and began it with a discussion of Whitman.

When I returned to Ohio for winter break, serendipity waited in the
mailbox: a letter from James Collins inviting me to contribute to a book
he was editing for Heinemann. The theme was the teaching and learning of language collaboratively. This was getting mystical. I sent Collins
the paper with an explanatory note. We shaped it to meet the needs of
the book. A year later the essay appeared in *Vital Signs 2: Teaching and
Learning Language Collaboratively* (Collins 1991).

Upon my return to UNH in January, I wrote my comprehensive
exam. It was an intensely fulfilling experience. Before I left UNH first
semester, I'd met with my committee—Tom Newkirk, Jane Hansen,
and Don Graves. We discussed areas of knowledge in reading and writing I would be asked questions about. Over the break Newkirk created
thirteen essay questions in three different categories. I would choose
eight of them to answer, at least two from each category.

It was a demanding, written test, no doubt. Newkirk asked each
question in such a way that stretched me. For instance, I believed fer-
vently in the importance of literacy across the curriculum. One chapter of *Clearing the Way* had been about using writing to think. Newkirk,
however, didn't just ask me to explain what I believed about writing
across the curriculum. He interjected a twist that pushed me to think
about the topic in a new way:

> Choose four authors who have influenced you most about how
> humans think and apply their philosophies and findings to the
> teaching of reading and writing across the curriculum.

What made the exam-writing experience so fulfilling were the
conditions that enabled me to think and write my best. Committee

members understood how writers worked, how varied were their writing processes. They extended that understanding to the graduate students. I was allowed to take the questions away and answer them in my own familiar place, in this case, the six-by-twelve dormitory room in Babcock with a wooden chair padded with a pillow and my computer set up on a card table. I had some choice in what I would write about. I had extended amounts of flexible time. I could draft an essay, put it aside, begin work on another, get it drafted, then revisit the previous essay with new eyes. It was a truncated process for the way I'd written *Clearing the Way*.

When I revisited an essay, I discovered garbled meaning, failed word choice, partial persuasions. Following fast on these realizations came alternate ways of saying, organizing, and arguing—"the second genius" (Stafford 2003, 36). I wrote eight essays like that, dividing my day into three writing sessions: morning, afternoon, and evening. Working Wednesday through Saturday, I produced sixty-seven double-spaced pages. Saturday night I went to a party at Jane Hansen's. I was tranquil, serene, not the least bit tired. I was in bed at the dorm by eleven and lay awake for hours, my mind still wired from the intellectual stimulation of the previous four days.

40

pure pleasure

That second semester we continued the reading and writing seminar that met at Graves' house. Portfolios were hot, and Don was excited about exploring their possibilities for learning and assessment. Next door, the state of Vermont was leading the nation in using portfolios to assess the writing skills of public school students. The seminar group dived into portfolios with Graves. We investigated the use of portfolios in other disciplines, particularly art. We talked about portfolios, kept portfolios, and shared articles. For the final project we all wrote articles about portfolios, pieces that Bonnie Sunstein and Don edited into a book that Heinemann published: *Portfolio Portraits* (Graves and Sunstein 1992).

For my second course that semester, Tom Newkirk had a suggestion. He knew I wanted to write young adult fiction. "Why don't you ask Murray to do an independent study with you?" Could I do that, I wondered? Murray had retired from teaching nearly three years earlier, though he was still a vital force in the UNH reading and writing community. His own writing flourished more than ever: books, articles, poetry, and a weekly column in the *Boston Globe*. The last summer he'd taught, 1987, I'd taken his fiction writing course, so he knew the territory I was mining. I asked Murray if he'd do an independent study with me.

He was reluctant. He was out of the UNH teaching scene, after all. This was tricky and complicated, he said. He didn't want to set a precedent. He wasn't sure. He didn't think so. He'd get back to me. He agreed.

I think that the tipping point was the chance he saw to have a regular live audience for his own fiction. He had been writing a novel with a central character named Blair, a World War II combat veteran, as he himself was. Each Wednesday we traded chapters we'd written. We read each other's work, wrote responses, and met on Thursday afternoons for an hour in his basement office at 39 Mill Pond Road in Durham, the New Hampshire woods outside the glass doors turning from snow-covered to green from January to May.

Murray titled his weekly piece for our independent study, "Romano Notes." In addition to responding to my writing, he discussed his own, and wrote about the craft of writing that he had been plying for decades. Our talks, stimulating and instructive, were about reading and writing fiction, our evolving novels—the discoveries we were making, the problems we were encountering, the plans we might try. And always we talked about teaching writing as well as writing writing. I left the weekly conference eager to write more.

The first three weeks, I gave Murray what I called draft-and-a-halfs, not my usual writing process. I was worried I wouldn't get the entire novel written in four months. I sped along from one half-baked idea to another. I'd draft a chapter, which often took two days. I'd reread it on the computer screen, tinker with it, then print.

"I don't think what you're giving me is representative of your best writing," Murray said.

It wasn't.

He asked about my usual writing process. I told him that I lived in revision. I engaged in multiple revisions of just about everything I wrote—three, five, sometimes as many as seven or eight revisions of something important. After each draft, I printed a copy, let it cool for at least a day, then revised by hand, tinkering, altering, deleting, adding, reconceiving. Then I typed in my revisions and printed another copy. I'd continue this cycle until the words stopped demanding to be changed.

Murray advised me to go back to that method. I did, with relief. By allowing more time and immersion in a chapter, everything improved. Detail sharpened. Characters gained complexity. Plot developed and tension heightened. I had more to think about both consciously and subconsciously. The increased process time let the fictional world build and grow. Imagining what came next became less stressful, almost inevitable. And because of this, I made more connections, saw more possibilities, began to understand more thoroughly what I was doing.

At the same time I wrote the novel, I was reading what novelists had to say about writing. Since he'd been a boy, Murray had paid attention to what writers wrote about the process of writing. He had countless recommendations for my reading. I read the *Paris Review* interviews with writers. I read articles. I read books.

When I needed to keep faith in my subject matter, I found Annie Dillard: "You were made and set here to give voice to this, our own astonishment" (Dillard 1989, 68).

When I despaired at the task of writing an entire novel, I had E. L. Doctorow: "[I]t's like driving a car at night. You never see further than your headlights, but you can make the whole trip that way" (quoted in Murray 1990, 100).

When I thought I was writing badly, I had William Stafford:

> The only standard I can rationally have is the standard I'm meeting right now. . . . You should be more willing to forgive yourself. It doesn't make any difference if you are good or bad today; the *assessment* of the product is something that happens *after* you've done it. (quoted in Murray 1990, 76)

When my autobiographical experience sabotaged the fiction I sought to create, I had Bernard Malamud: "I prefer autobiographical essence to autobiographical history. Events from life may creep into the narrative but it isn't necessarily my life history" (quoted in Stern 1983, 51).

Murray had suggested that I keep a journal of my creative process as I wrote the novel. I liked the idea. I had been reading John Steinbeck's journals and letters that he'd written while writing *The Grapes of Wrath* and *East of Eden*. Steinbeck wrote *before* he began producing his daily quota of fiction, often discussing what he would write about, the journal writing warming him to the fiction writing. I wrote *after* writing fiction. I sought to capture my writing processes and creative moves, my invention strategies and dilemmas, all the slick spots and sloughs of writing the novel. I wanted to make the invisible visible, to reveal the nuances of the process that were easily forgotten. I gave these journal entries to Murray each week, along with the fiction. He soon convinced me that I had a dissertation topic in the work I was doing and the data I was gathering—the many drafts of chapters, the journal, the reading into the creative process. My dissertation became a self-reflective analysis of the creation of a young adult novel.

In May of 1991, I graduated with my doctorate. Six members of my family traveled from Ohio to New Hampshire for the graduation ceremony held on the UNH football field, folding chairs set up on the grass, a dais erected near one end zone. It was hot, muggy, and overcast, uncharacteristic weather, really, for southern New Hampshire that time of year. I removed my shirt and fittingly wore a New Hampshire Literacy Institute T-shirt under my graduation robe.

All the prospective graduates for various degrees were lined up, ready to march down a grassy aisle amid the folding chairs. The band struck up "Pomp and Circumstance" and caught me off guard. I felt my ears go red. My goodness. This was a big moment. As I walked toward our chairs in front, I saw my mother standing next to the aisle, looking toward me as I approached. She was seventy-six years old, slight, and osteoperotic. She had her hair done every week and was rarely without a cigarette. She had quit school in May of her ninth grade year. She had talked about my getting a college education since I was a boy. She became determined that would happen after Red was killed. The music swelled. Mom's bottom lip trembled. Tears streamed down her cheeks. She was fierce. She was proud.

It's been seventeen years now since Tom Newkirk hooded me that grey, muggy morning on the football field. The University of New Hampshire has meant a great deal to me. UNH meant Don Murray and Tom Newkirk, Don Graves, Jane Hansen, and my fellow graduate students. UNH meant Jan Roberts and her third graders at Mast Way, who would be in their thirties now. UNH meant my New Hampshire Literacy Institute friends—Linda Rief, Maureen Barbieri, Susan Stires, and Jack Wilde. UNH meant all that time I'd spent with language, all that reading, and more importantly, all that writing. Writing and teaching writing had come to define my life.

In workshops, in classes, in my office in McGuffey Hall at Miami University, the name UNH often comes up some way. Maybe I'll refer to the Literacy Institute. Maybe a student will mention my UNH lamp or UNH director's chair. Maybe they'll see a framed photo of Don Murray and me. When I mention the University of New Hampshire, I genuflect. People are surprised and smile. They figure I'm kidding. I am. I'm half kidding. I'm all serious.

Epilog
almost there

When our daughter, Mariana, was two and a half, her favorite play space was the kitchen floor. She pulled plastic storage bowls out of a cabinet and began stacking and building. Kathy and I were required to step around a floor cluttered with her inventive, purposeful play. She was an utter delight at that age, spouting language and living in metaphor. "Get your pipe and blow doughnuts," she once commanded me.

Her potty training was progressing, too. She had learned to use without fail a pink, hand-me-down potty chair—for number one, that is. She wasn't so successful with bowel movements. Mariana always told us about them, but only *after* she'd had one. She meant to get to the potty chair, but never quite made it.

We know the old saying repeated after someone's flawed attempt. A cynic will utter, "The road to hell is paved with good intentions."

As a teacher, I relish watching my students travel that road. You give me a student willing to try with all she's got, and I am in pedagogical heaven. My students at Miami University are studying to be English teachers. The first lessons they plan and teach are often a mix of good and bad. They'll have solid information, but assume too much about what their students know. They'll show flashes of creativity, but their classroom presence might be nervous and tentative. I expect this mix of strengths and weaknesses. My students are learning. After they teach their lessons, I get them to talk about what went well, what surprised them, and what they'll do differently next time. In many ways, it is just like a writing conference with the students reflecting on the teaching draft they've submitted.

Teachers are sometimes criticized for having low standards and inflating grades. They need to care more about quality, we hear; they need to be held accountable. I suppose I am one of those teachers, even though I love quality teaching and quality writing. I know that by semester's end my students' presence in front of a class will be confident. Their lessons will be imaginative and interesting. They will start with what their students know and build from there. Yes, quality and fine performance always get my admiration.

But I am a teacher. I know that the path toward accomplishment can be a zigzag one, replete with setbacks, wrong turns, and backtracking. That's why I value approximation so much: the flawed attempt, the good intentions gone awry, the achievement of *approximately* what you were after. For those who participate in good faith, learning is a matter of growth and development. It took me years to get this understanding into my own teaching philosophy, even though our daughter had demonstrated it right under my nose.

One afternoon as Mariana played on the kitchen floor, Kathy stopped short and looked down at something odd. "Oh, Tom," she called. "You've got to see this." She directed my attention to one of the plastic bowls. What on earth . . . oh my! Mariana had exercised quick, associative thinking. I marveled at her toddler logic. The bowl was white, not pink. But it was plastic and just the right size. I imagined our delightful, curly-haired daughter a minute or two earlier feeling the peristaltic urge, moving swiftly to squat over the bowl, and, without so much as a grunt, completing the digestive cycle.

Oh, yes, I value approximation, whether it is a twenty-year-old learning to teach, a toddler learning the civilities of bathroom etiquette, or myself finding my way as a reader, writer, teacher, and learner.

Works Cited

Allen, Camille. 2001. *The Multigenre Research Paper: Voice, Passion, and Discovery in Grades 4–6*. Portsmouth, NH: Heinemann.

Atwell, Nancy. 1987. *In the Middle: Writing, Reading, and Learning with Adolescents*. Upper Montclair, NJ: Boynton/Cook.

Csikszentmihalyi, Mihaly. 1990. *Flow: The Psychology of Optimal Experience*. New York: Harper & Row.

Collins, James, ed. 1991. *Vital Signs 2: Teaching and Learning Language Collaboratively*. Portsmouth, NH: Boynton/Cook.

Dickinson, Emily. 1961 [1890]. *Final Harvest: Emily Dickinson's Poems*. Selection and Introduction by Thomas H. Johnson. Boston: Little, Brown and Company.

Dillard, Annie. 1989. *The Writing Life*. New York: Harper & Row.

Edmundson, Mark. 2004. *Why Read?* New York: Bloomsbury.

Elbow, Peter. 1973. *Writing Without Teachers*. New York: Oxford University Press.

Emig, Janet. 1971. *The Composing Processes of Twelfth Graders*. Urbana, IL: NCTE.

Fader, Daniel N., and Elton B. McNeil. 1968. *Hooked on Books: Program & Proof*. New York: Berkley Publishing Corporation.

Gabori, George. 1981. *When Evils Were Most Free*. Toronto: Seal Books.

Gilligan, Carol. 1982. *In a Different Voice: Psychological Theory and Women's Development*. Cambridge, MA: Harvard University Press.

Graves, Donald H. 1983. *Writing: Teachers and Children at Work*. Portsmouth, NH: Heinemann.

Graves, Donald H., and Jane Hansen. 1983. "The Author's Chair." *Language Arts* 60 (February): 176–83.

Graves, Donald H., and Bonnie Sunstein, eds. 1992. *Portfolio Portraits*. Portsmouth, NH: Heinemann.

Kaplan, Justin. 1980. *Walt Whitman: A Life*. New York: Bantam.

Lamott, Anne. 1994. *Bird by Bird: Some Instructions on Writing and Life*. New York: Pantheon Books.

Lee, Harper. 1960. *To Kill a Mockingbird*. Philadephia: Lippincott.

London, Jack. [1904] 1965. *The Sea Wolf*. Clinton, MA: The Colonial Press, Inc.

Macrorie, Ken. 1976. *Writing to Be Read*. 2d rev. ed. Rochelle Park, NJ: Hayden Book Co.

Murray, Donald. 1982. "Teaching the Other Self." In *Learning by Teaching: Selected Articles on Writing and Teaching*. Portsmouth, NH: Boynton/Cook.

———. 1984. *Write to Learn*. New York: CBS College Publishing.

———. 1985. "Writing Badly to Write Well: Searching for the Instructive Line." In *Sentence Combining: A Rhetorical Perspective*, eds. Donald A. Daiker, Andrew Kerek, and Max Morenberg. Carbondale and Edwardsville: Southern Illinois University Press.

———. 1989. *Expecting the Unexpected: Teaching Myself—and Others—to Write*. Portsmouth, NH: Boynton/Cook–Heinemann.

———. 1990. *Shoptalk: Learning to Write with Writers*. Portsmouth, NH: Boynton/Cook–Heinemann.

Neilsen, Lorri. 1998. *Knowing Her Place: Research Literacies and Feminist Occasions*. San Francisco: Caddo Gap Press.

Newkirk, Thomas. 1989. *More Than Stories: The Range of Children's Writing*. Portsmouth, NH: Heinemann.

Ondaatje, Michael. 1984. *The Collected Works of Billy the Kid*. New York: Penguin. 1970. Original edition. Toronto: House of Anansi Press.

Putz, Melinda. 2006. *A Teacher's Guide to the Multigenre Research Project: Everything You Need to Get Started*. Portsmouth, NH: Heinemann.

Romano, Tom. 1985. "Eight Children Teach Donald Graves." *Language Arts* 62 (2): 142.

———. 1987. *Clearing the Way: Working with Teenage Writers*. Portsmouth, NH: Heinemann.

———. 1990. "A Conversation with Robert Cormier." In *To Compose: Teaching Writing in High School and College*, ed. Thomas Newkirk. Portsmouth, NH: Boynton/Cook–Heinemann.

———. 1991. "Writing Through Others: The Necessity of Collaboration." In *Vital Signs 2: Teaching and Learning Language Collaboratively*, ed. James L. Collins. Portsmouth, NH: Boynton/Cook.

———. 1995. *Writing with Passion: Life Stories, Multiple Genres*. Portsmouth, NH: Heinemann.

———. 2000. *Blending Genre, Altering Style: Writing Multigenre Papers*. Portsmouth, NH: Heinemann.

Rose, Mike. 1989. *Lives on the Boundary: The Struggles and Achievements of America's Underprepared*. New York: The Free Press.

Stafford, Kim. 2003. *The Muses Among Us: Eloquent Listening and Other Pleasures of the Writer's Craft*. Athens, GA: The University of Georgia Press.

Stern, Daniel. 1983. "A Conversation with Bernard Malamud." In *First Person Singular: Writers on Their Craft*, compiled by Joyce Carol Oates. Princeton, NJ: Ontario Review Press.

Weathers, Winston. 1980. *An Alternate Style: Options in Composition*. Rochelle Park, NJ: Hayden Book Company. Distributed by Heinemann, Portsmouth, NH. OP

Whitman, Walt. [1855] 1981. *Leaves of Grass*. Franklin Center, PA: The Franklin Library.

Acknowledgments for borrowed material continued from page ii:

"Coming to Teaching" by Tom Romano was originally published in *English Journal* (Volume 97, Number 2, 2007). Copyright © 2007 by the National Council of Teachers of English. Reprinted with permission.

"Living Literature" by Tom Romano was originally published in *English Journal* (Volume 91, Number 3, 2002). Copyright © 2002 by the National Council of Teachers of English. Reprinted with permission.

"Censorship and the Student Voice" by Tom Romano was originally published in *English Journal* (Volume 67, Number 5, 1978). Copyright © 1978 by the National Council of Teachers of English. Reprinted with permission.

"Eight Children Teach Donald Graves" by Tom Romano was originally published in *Language Arts* (Volume 62, Number 2, 1985). Copyright © 1985 by the National Council of Teachers of English. Reprinted with permission.

Gratitudes

’m aware of many people who influenced the creation of *Zigzag*. I express my gratitude to them here. There are many folks, though, who have contributed to my thinking in ways I have forgotten or am unaware of. Sometimes their stories, reactions, or bits of information altered my perceptions, clarified ideas, or spurred journal entries. Bless you all, you anonymous helpers.

Below are the companions my words had that I do know about. "Grazie, grazie," I say to them all. *Grazie*.

The Heinemann team is a remarkable one. Lisa Luedeke has been my editor on two books now. When my initial concept was nebulous, she saw through the murk to possibility.

Leah Peake has been editorial director at Heinemann since 1997. She's got everything a captain needs: intellect, vitality, steadiness, and courage.

At one point, Managing Editor Maura Sullivan entered the bookmaking process and moved it along swiftly. Maura is all substance.

Vicki Kasabian, my production editor, dived in with all her intellect and heart. She attended to details both technical and emotional and made me one happy author.

In her own words, Promotions Coordinator Doria Turner does "all kinds of stuff." I'm glad she was doing some of that stuff for *Zigzag*. Copywriter Eric Chalek produces language in a passionate sweep, then listens, adjusts, and drafts anew to create enticing back cover copy. Denise Botelho copyedited the surface of my words with a light, exacting touch. And Roberta Lew, Heinemann's Tsar of Permissions, is savvy, careful, and covers all bases.

Judy Arisman designed the cover of *Zigzag*, which is the fourth time I've been blessed with her aesthetic sensibility. Look at *Writing with Passion*, published thirteen years ago, to understand why. The first time I saw that cover, I was so instantly moved that my knees buckled.

My students sometimes refer to Miami University as "Mother Miami." I did that myself when I was a student here forty-one years ago. Miami has certainly been a mother to me. It has nurtured my creativity and enabled my productivity by granting me three leaves since 1995 to write books. Mother has been happy with the outcome; so have I.

Linsey Milillo was my graduate assistant and student in two classes. Linsey suggested a phrase for the Epilog that struck just the right note of civility and, thus, helped me achieve the ping. She is also a whiz on the computer.

Bill Pratt, emeritus professor of English at Miami University, directed me to the precise Emily Dickinson poem that prompted my final exam essay in freshmen English in 1968. The man has a memory for literature.

Tact, Hitash, and Richard—the tech support guys in Miami's School of Education, Health, and Society—teach with expertise and patience to both the techno natives and immigrants (that is, those of us who came to technology late and have never quite become fluent).

Masha Misco and Stacy Nakamura Brinkman are librarians at Miami University. These women love the hunt.

Gary Scott, news director at WMUB (88.5 FM) in Oxford, is a musician, consummate word man, and expert at getting writers to say what they need.

Don Daiker is now retired from Miami after more than four decades of teaching. Imagine that! A number of students he taught retired before he did. Don remembered the Q-Test in freshmen English and details of those sentence-combining conferences at Miami University in the 1970s and 1980s that inspired so many of us.

Barry Witham taught my theatre course in 1971. Barry did what no other teacher had ever done in my presence. He opened his soul and revealed how a literary text was about more than plot, characters, themes, and blue books.

I had some fine minds weigh in on one chapter when I asked for help: Maja Wilson, Penny Kittle, and Barb Heuberger sharpened my understanding.

I've visited a number of National Writing Project sites across the country. I thank them for invitations to work with their teachers. I particularly thank Mary Fuller, director of the Ohio Writing Project at Miami. A golden soul is she.

Kathy and I both extend appreciation to Phyllis Mendenhall. She has been a steadfast friend since we returned to Ohio. Phyllis has a keen sense of irreverence and is quick to provide bawdy humor. She is also a wizard in her role as chief advisor of my Department of Teacher Education. It figures that a Kansas girl would be into wizardry.

I wrote a lot about Red's Nite Club, my father's bar and bowling alleys, known in the family as "the place." At Red's you could count on a good sandwich, a cold bottle of pop or draft beer, air conditioning, and camaraderie. I thank all of my father's customers, most of them long past now—the bowlers, bullshitters, advisors, occasional bullies and curmudgeons, Italian immigrants, brickyard and steel mill workers, and more alcoholics, I'm afraid, than I realized as a boy. I have fond memories, though, of just about all of them.

Joey Thompson was my first friend, going back to a sunny time behind Mr. Red's place in the early 1950s. Joey might call me too late at night sometimes, but my love for him soon clears the cobwebs of sleep.

Bill Monroe and Brenda Kirby Coe were classmates of mine from grade school through high school. They demonstrated courage and an active sense of social justice. I thank them. I also thank Karen Wackerly. She and her late husband—my longtime friend, Danny Wackerly—shared their memories with me and illuminated the past about things I did not know.

Brian McKnight is an actor, a director, and a former student of mine twenty years ago at Edgewood High School in Trenton, Ohio. One bleak winter day after school, Brian walked beside me as I left my classroom for my car, playing his guitar, serenading me with one Beatles' song after another. As a mere teenager Brian took the multigenre idea

I introduced and demonstrated achievement I hadn't imagined. We need more men like Brian in this country.

Phyllis Neumann was my mentor teacher when I student taught at Edgewood in 1970. She's been a friend ever since. Would that my present students at Miami have as good a student teaching experience as I had with Phyllis. What a career launch for them that would be.

Nancy McDonald is my beloved sister, the woman I've known longest on this earth. Nancy's thoughtfulness, kindness, and humor have enhanced the lives of many. In so doing, she has reaped much love. Her role in this book was a crucial one. She told me about her perceptions of the night our father died and swiftly filled in a blank in my memory that had existed for forty-three years.

The most photogenic Leah Mae Romano Furney is our granddaughter. Her parents, Todd Furney and Mariana Romano, conceived a gem of a child in her. They continue the successful collaboration, raising Leah Mae amid love, responsibility, and a dynamic political mix of Democratic ideals, Republican conservatism, and feminist strength.

Kathy Romano—my spouse, lover, and friend of thirty-eight years— is the great mainmast of our family. She snapped three candid photographs I'll never forget.

I am grateful to the many permutations of my journal over the last thirty-five years. It has been a storehouse of memory, thought, ramblings, flashes of brilliance, joy, surprise, and occasional desperation. Many of the observations, stories, and chapters in *Zigzag* began first in the journal. The clearest, simplest advice I can give to those who want to write is to buy a journal they'd enjoy writing in. Make regular dates with it. Keep them. The relationship will grow.

Kathy and I spent four years in Logan, Utah, in Cache Valley, where I taught in a terrific English department at Utah State University. We had to leave Utah, but our lives changed for the better because of that stay. We travel to Cache Valley each year to spend time with folks we love. Here are six of them:

Carol Strong, Dean of the School of Education at USU, and Bill Strong, emeritus professor now and still a leading language arts educator for over thirty-five years. Bill and Carol's MO is taste, wit, intellect, and warmth.

Will and Teri Pitkin open the Hotel Pitkin to Kathy and me for extended stays. Each visit they throw a Romano Party so we can see other Cache Valley friends in one convivial gathering. We have laughed aplenty at the Pitkins' home, a brand of ribald humor that would have made Shakespeare grin and pipe up.

Ken Brewer was a longtime member of the USU English department. When he died in March 2006, he was Utah's poet laureate and at the top of his game as a writer. In the fifteen years of our friendship Ken influenced my teaching and writing as much as anyone. Kathy and I miss him. Ken's widow, Bobbie Stearman, remains our friend and fellow lover of schnauzers, particularly Max, Murray, Minnie Mae, Jasmine, Hemingway, Gus, and Gretchen.

Don Murray died December 30, 2006. For twenty-three years he was my friend and mentor, a real mensch of the written word. I was two weeks into writing *Zigzag* when he died. Months before his death, I placed a photo near my computer of Don and Kathy taken during dinner one evening at Maureen and Richie Barbieri's in Kittery Point, Maine. Each morning as I wrote, Don's spirit and writerly discipline were with me. May they always be.